TREES

OF BRITAIN AND EUROPE

TREES

OF BRITAIN AND EUROPE

ELIZABETH MARTIN

Illustrated by
Norma Birgin and Terry Callcut

Consultant
Alan Mitchell

Kingfisher Books · London

First published in 1978.
This edition published in 1983 by Kingfisher Books Limited
Elsley Court, 20–22 Great Titchfield Street, London W1P 7AD

© Kingfisher Books Limited 1978

BRITISH LIBRARY CATALOGUING IN PUBLICATION DATA
Martin, Elizabeth
  Trees. Kingfisher guide to trees of Britain
  and Europe. – (Kingfisher guides)
  1. Trees – Europe
  I. Title   II. Kingfisher guide to trees
  of Britain and Europe
  582.16094   QK487
  ISBN 0 86272 056 7

Edited by Sonya Larkin
Colour separations by Newsele Litho, Milan, London
Printed and bound in Italy by Vallardi Industrie
Grafiche, Milan

CONTENTS

INTRODUCTION

Trees are defined as woody plants, at least 6m tall, with a single main stem (*trunk*) that divides into branches (forming the *crown*) some distance above the ground. Shrubs are smaller woody plants with several stems that divide from ground level. Both trees and shrubs are *perennials* – they do not die down in winter. Most of the plants described in this book are trees in the strict sense of the word, but a few shrubs are included, either because they are very common or because they sometimes attain tree size and/or habit.

Trees and shrubs do not form a single botanical group. They are divided into *conifers*, *palms*, and *broad-leaved trees*. Conifers produce cones instead of flowers; they are usually (but not always) evergreen and they have narrow leaves. Both palms and broad-leaved trees are flowering plants, but the palms do not produce true wood or bark. All these trees are further subdivided into *families*, *genera* (singular: *genus*), and *species*. Plants of the same family share some characteristics but are not as closely related as plants of the same genus or species. For example, the family *Rosaceae* contains herbaceous plants, as well as trees and shrubs, and they all have similar flowers. Within this family are many genera of trees: *Crataegus* (haw-thorns), *Prunus* (cherries, almonds, peaches), etc., which are divided into species. The genus *Sorbus*, for example, contains the species *S. aria* (white-beam), *S. aucuparia* (rowan), and *S. domestica* (service tree).

The trees in this book are grouped in the order in which they are classified by botanists: first conifers, then palms, and finally broad-leaved trees. They are all subdivided into their family groups to give some idea of the relationships between the different genera.

Parts of a Tree

Like other plants, trees bear leaves, flowers, and fruit. The shape, size, and colour of the leaves are an important means of identification. The leaf of a broad-leaved tree is typically flat and has a large surface area. It contains the green pigment *chlorophyll* and its surface is dotted with microscopic pores (*stomata*). Leaves have several functions. They manufacture food (carbohydrate) from carbon dioxide (taken in through the stomata) and water (absorbed by the roots), using energy in the form of sunlight, which is trapped

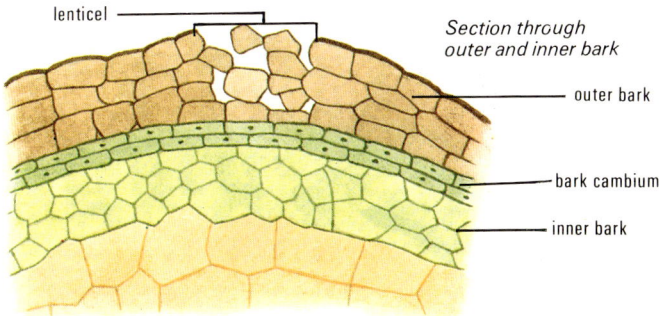

lenticel

Section through outer and inner bark

outer bark

bark cambium

inner bark

Reflected glory – a view of trees by a lake.

by the chlorophyll. This process is called *photosynthesis*. A tree absorbs more water than it can use, and the excess is lost through the stomata of the leaves in *transpiration*. A tree can also breathe through its leaves. Oxygen is taken in through the stomata and used for the breakdown (oxidation) of food in other parts of the tree to release the energy needed for growth and other vital processes.

Deciduous trees shed all their leaves at the same time every year so that their branches are bare in winter. Such trees, which are usually broad-leaved, grow in regions with marked seasonal changes in climate. The absence of leaves greatly reduces loss of water from the tree during the harsh winter months. *Evergreens*, on the other hand, never have bare branches: they lose, and replace, their leaves periodically but never all at the same time. Most conifers are evergreens. They are found in the colder regions, and in order to take advantage of the short summer season do not waste time in producing a complete new set of leaves each year. In winter the stomata of their leaves close, which prevents loss of water from the tree.

Flowers are the reproductive organs of the tree. They contain stamens, which produce pollen (containing the male sex cells) and a pistil (containing the ovules, which develop into seeds). A flower cannot produce seeds until it is fertilized by pollen. In order for this to take place the flower must be pollinated; that is, pollen must be placed on the stigma. The size, structure, colour, and scent of a flower all help to ensure that pollination takes place, and the variety of flower structure in trees reflects the different ways in which they are pollinated. The flowers of the cherry, hawthorn, and related trees have conspicuous petals and are often scented (see diagram): this attracts insects, which act as pollinating agents. Such trees as the oak, beech, and elm have small and inconspicuous flowers, often lacking petals. In these trees the pollen is transported by wind.

After fertilization, the ovary of the flower develops into the fruit, which contains the seeds. Again, there is great variation in the types of fruit produced by trees. Some form fleshy fruits (apple, pear, cherry); others produce nuts (chestnut, beech, oak, hazel); pods (laburnum, wattle); winged fruits (ash, maple); and so on.

The cones of conifers have the same function as the flowers of palms and broad-leaved trees. Separate male and female cones are produced, the females (after fertilization) developing into the familiar woody or leathery structures containing the seeds.

How Trees Grow

Trees grow in length by division of the cells at the tips of their shoots; they grow in thickness by the production of wood. The trunk of a broad-leaved tree contains a series of thick-walled tubes called *xylem vessels*. These vessels form the wood of the tree: they carry water and mineral salts absorbed by the roots to the branches, and they also strengthen the trunk and branches. Outside the xylem is another set of tubes – the *phloem* (or *bast*) – which transports food made in the leaves to the rest of the tree. Both these tissues are produced by a thin layer of cells called the *cambium*. The amount of xylem produced by a broad-leaved tree varies within a single season. In spring – a period of intensive growth in which the tree needs a lot of water – a large number of big xylem vessels are formed (the *spring wood*). In summer and autumn smaller vessels are produced, and in winter all growth ceases. This cycle of growth is repeated the following year. A single year's growth of wood can be seen in a cross-section of the trunk as an *annual ring*, and the number of annual rings indicates the age of the tree. In older trees only the outer annual rings contain functional xylem: this is the *sapwood*. The centre of the trunk is made up of dead xylem vessels, known as *heartwood*, which is often darker in colour as it is impregnated with tannins or resins. *Medullary rays*, which contribute to the grain of some timbers, are lines of living thin-walled cells through which food is transported across the xylem vessels.

The Bark

Outside the phloem is another layer of cambium – the *bark cambium*. From its outer surface it divides to produce corky cells, of which the bark is formed. The bark provides an impermeable layer that protects the tree against attack by disease-causing bacteria and fungi; prevents the entry of water, which would cause rotting; and reduces water loss from the tree. However, in order for the tree to breathe, the bark is broken at intervals by tiny pores called *lenticels*. These are large enough to allow air to enter but small enough to prevent loss of water from the tree. The colour and texture of the bark and lenticels is an important means of identification for some trees.

Evolution and Distribution

Every species of tree has its own area of natural distribution. The climate, soil, and other factors that influence tree

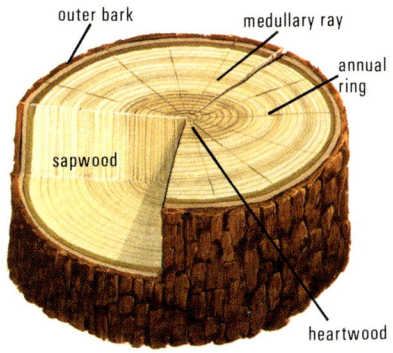

Section through tree trunk

growth are, in such areas, particularly favourable for the growth of the trees that are found there. The differences (variations) between species are the result of adaptation to different environments. Variations result from mutations (changes in the characteristics of the tree). If a mutation improves the chances of survival of a tree in a particular environment and is inheritable, it will be passed on to the offspring of that tree, which will also thrive if environmental conditions re-

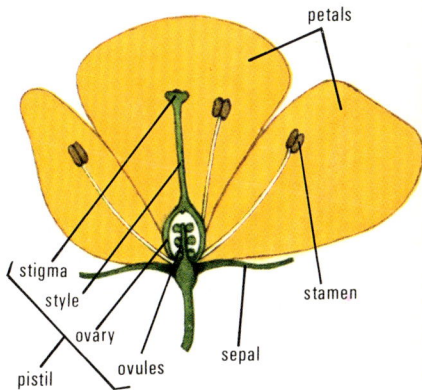

Section through typical flower

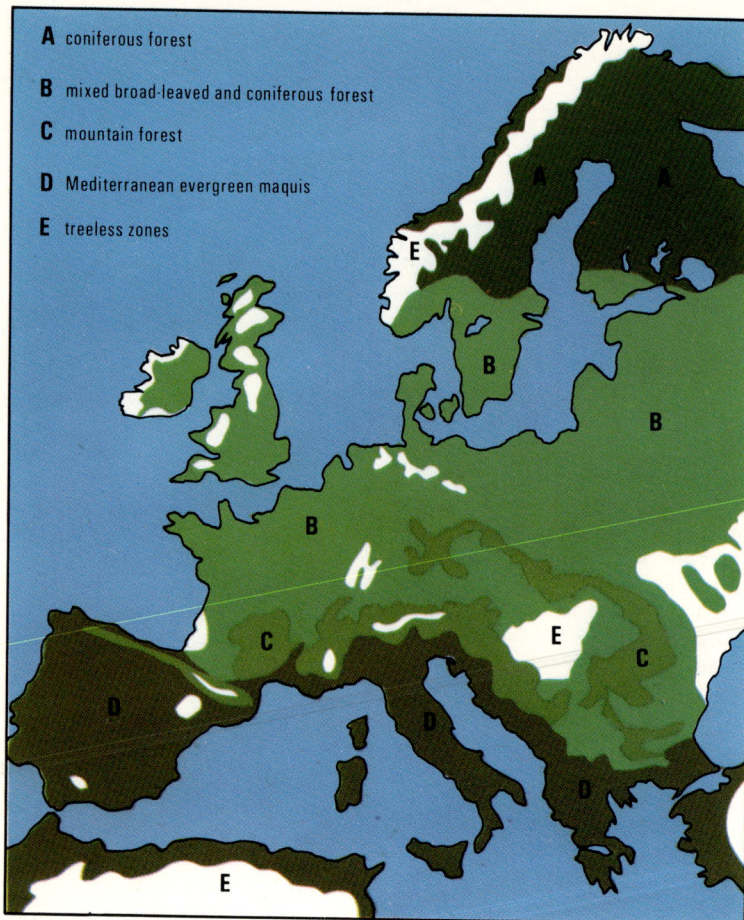

A coniferous forest

B mixed broad-leaved and coniferous forest

C mountain forest

D Mediterranean evergreen maquis

E treeless zones

Distribution of Forests and Woodlands in Europe

main the same. As the environment gradually changes over the years the trees change with it, adapting to new conditions by developing the appropriate variations.

The pattern of natural distribution of European trees seen today is the result of adaptation to an environment that has been profoundly affected by the last Ice Age (which began about one million years ago). As the ice extended south from the polar regions the trees growing at that time in northern Europe were gradually pushed south in front of it. When the ice retreated (the last retreat occurred some 11,000 years ago), the trees – when they could – spread back northwards again. In Europe the chain of mountains formed by the Pyrenees, Alps, and Carpathians produced a barrier from east to west that effectively prevented many trees from returning to their former northern habitats. Trees such as the Austrian pine are to this day restricted to the cool mountainous regions of southern Europe.

The distribution of European forests and woodlands seen today is shown in the map on p. 11. Conifers are mostly restricted to the more northerly parts of Europe, extending into the Arctic Circle, but isolated forests are found on southern mountains. The large area of deciduous forest that formerly extended over the whole of central and western Europe has been greatly reduced by man's intensive cultivation schemes, especially in western Europe. Large areas of forest have been cleared for the planting of cereals and other crops, and this part of Europe is today a mixture of woodland and grassland. A similar pattern can be seen in the south.

Identification of Trees

Most people would be able to distinguish between a palm, a conifer, and a broad-leaved tree. The general outline of a palm – with its straight unbranched stem topped by a crown of large leaves – is unmistakable. A closer inspection of the stem would reveal an outer covering of fibres, rather than bark (as in conifers and broad-leaves). A conifer, too, can usually be recognized by its outline (often tall and conical); also by its leaves (usually evergreen, either needles or fernlike fronds made up of scales) and its cones. To distinguish between the different kinds of conifers and broad-leaved trees is a more difficult task. Leaves provide the most reliable means of

identification. The most common conifers and broad-leaved trees may be identified, on the basis of their leaf structure, by reference to the text below and to the keys on the following pages.

Conifers

Needle-like leaves
 Needles in bunches of 2, 3, or 5: *pines*
 Needles in clusters on spurs:
  evergreen: *cedars*
  deciduous: *larches*
Needles borne singly:
 soft and flexible: *Douglas fir*
 flattened, of different lengths: *hemlocks*
 arranged in 2 rows along the stem:
  dark green with notched tips: *firs*
  very dark green and flattened: *yew*
  pointed; dark green above, white lines beneath: *redwood*
growing from pegs all round the stem: *spruces*
 arranged in whorls of 3 round the stem: *junipers*
Scalelike leaves
 overlapping each other to cover the branchlets completely: *cypresses*, *western red cedar*

Broad-leaved Trees

The leaves of these trees are extremely variable, and the types illustrated here do not cover all the species described in this book. Most of the genera are represented by the leaf of a single species: reference should be made to the text articles for identification of the other species of a particular genus. The leaves illustrated here are divided into 3 broad groups: *compound leaves* (made up of 2 or more leaflets); *simple leaves – lobed*; and *simple leaves – unlobed* (with smooth or toothed margins).

Compound Leaves

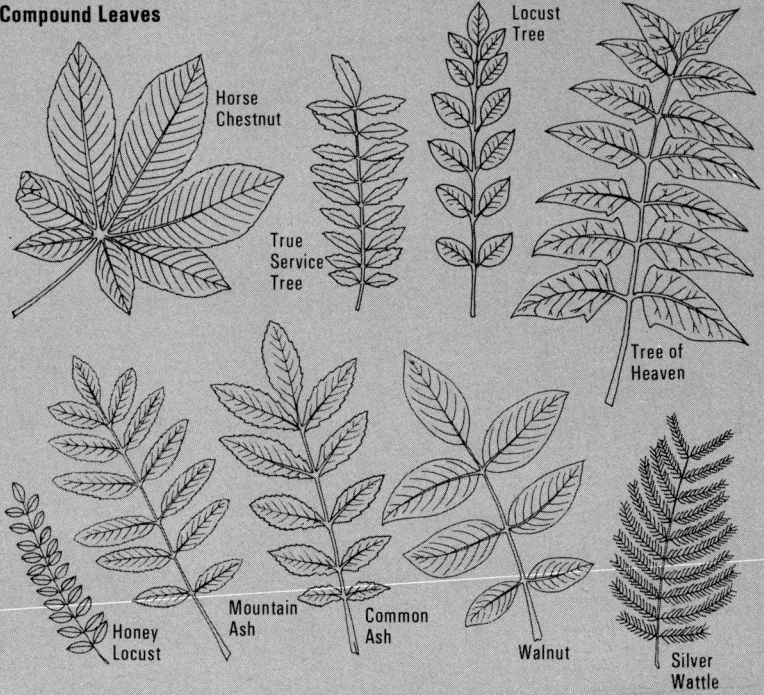

Horse Chestnut

Locust Tree

True Service Tree

Tree of Heaven

Honey Locust

Mountain Ash

Common Ash

Walnut

Silver Wattle

Simple Leaves – Lobed

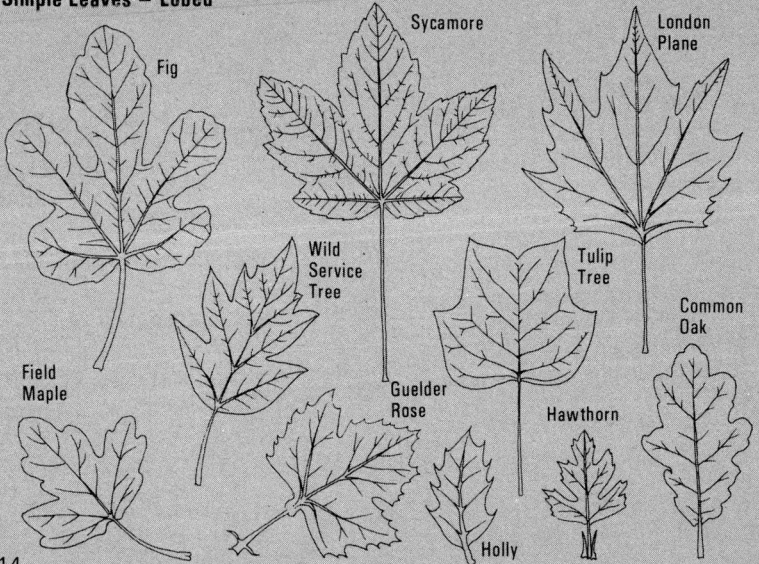

Fig

Sycamore

London Plane

Wild Service Tree

Tulip Tree

Common Oak

Field Maple

Guelder Rose

Hawthorn

Holly

Simple Leaves — Unlobed

Sweet Chestnut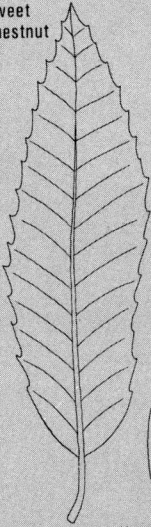

Beech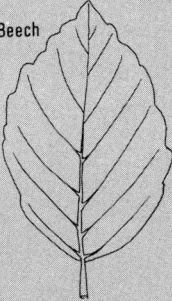

Wych Elm

Common Alder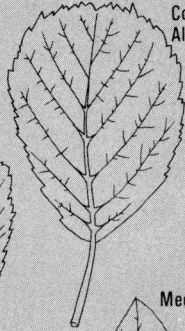

Judas Tree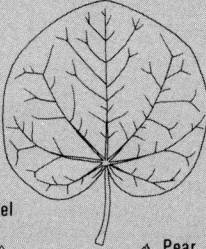

Hornbeam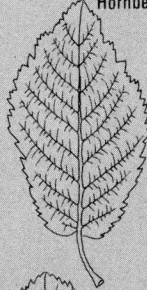

Medlar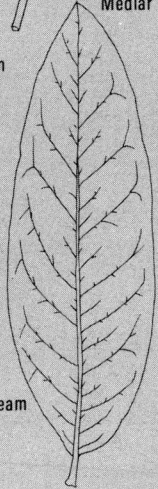

Hazel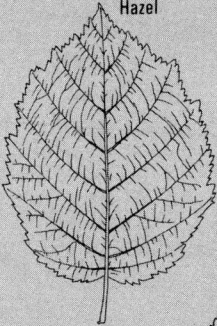

Pear

Whitebeam

Common Lime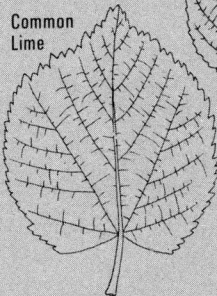

Apple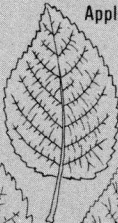

Silver Birch

Almond

Crack Willow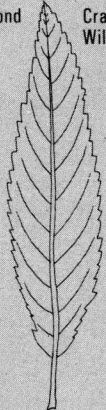

Wayfaring Tree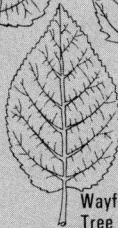

Black Mulberry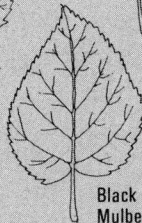

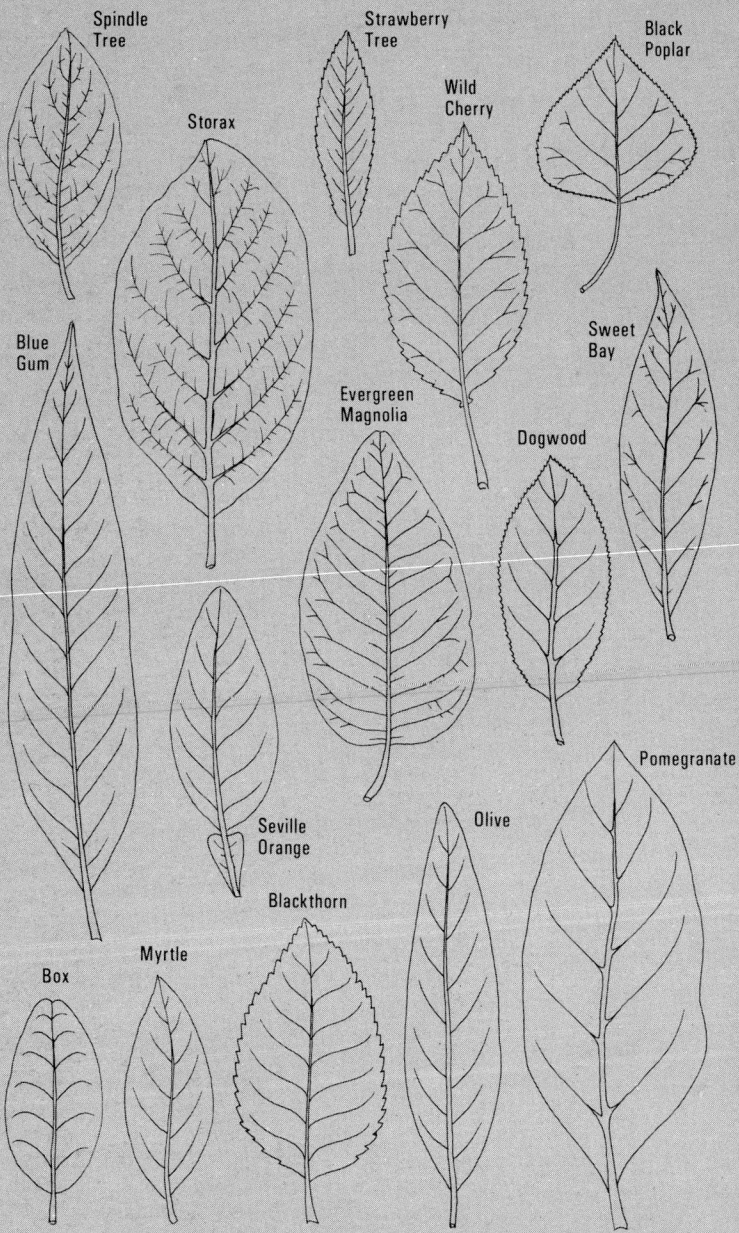

Spindle Tree

Strawberry Tree

Black Poplar

Wild Cherry

Storax

Blue Gum

Sweet Bay

Evergreen Magnolia

Dogwood

Pomegranate

Seville Orange

Olive

Blackthorn

Box

Myrtle

Types of Cones

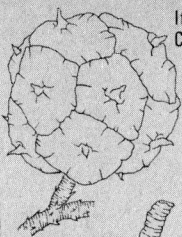

Italian Cypress

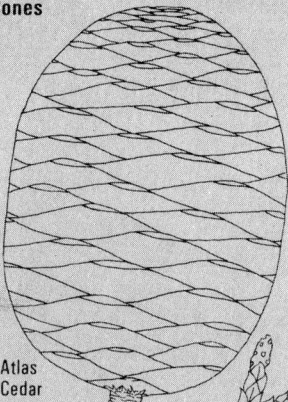

Atlas Cedar

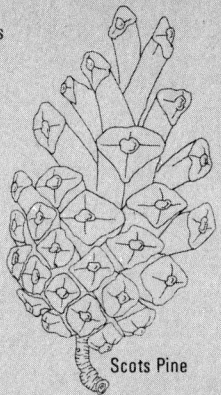

Scots Pine

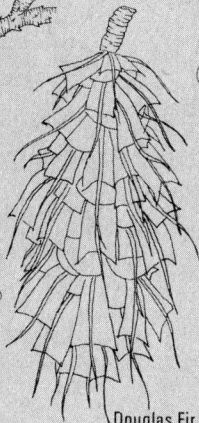

Douglas Fir

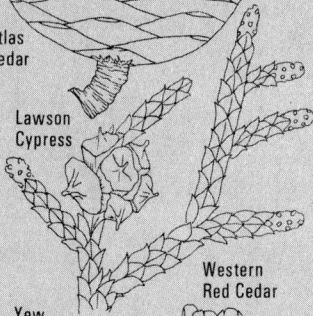

Lawson Cypress

Western Red Cedar

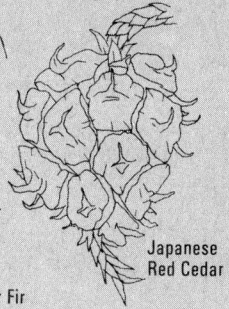

Japanese Red Cedar

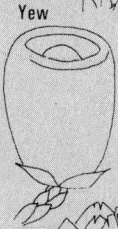

Yew

Silver Fir

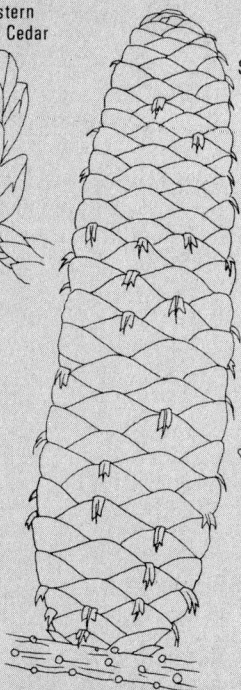

Dawn Redwood

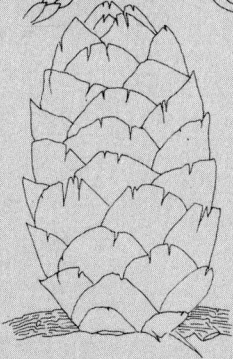

European Larch

Juniper

17

PINE FAMILY *(Pinaceae)*

This important family of over 200 species occurs in the Northern hemisphere, forming forests in the cooler northern regions and restricted to mountains in the south. The trees belonging to it – firs, cedars, larches, spruces, pines, and hemlocks – all have needle-like leaves and woody cones made up of spirally arranged scales.

SILVER FIR *(Abies alba)*

This European conifer forms pure forests in mountainous regions of central Europe, from the Pyrenees across the Alps to the Balkan mountains. It is widely cultivated for its timber and other useful products and it grows to 55m.

Crown: narrow and conical, with level branches that have upturned tips

Bark: smooth, dark grey, and blistered in young trees, becoming cracked into small square plates with age.
Shoots: grey-buff, with dark hairs.
Buds: red-brown and egg-shaped.
Leaves: thick needles with notched tips, dark green above with two narrow white bands beneath; 2–2·5cm long. They are arranged in two rows along the twigs.
Cones: erect and cylindrical, 10–15cm long, ripening from green to orange-brown. The large scales have bracts turned towards the base of the cone; they fall off when ripe leaving a central axis on the tree.
Uses: soft yellow-white timber best for planks, joinery, boxes, carving, paper pulp, etc. Oil of turpentine, distilled from the leaves and wood, is

natural
distribution
of silver fir

Silver Fir

mature
female
cone

used in medicine and veterinary work for sprains and bruises; Strasbourg turpentine, obtained from the bark blisters, is used in paints and varnishes.

Giant Fir

mature
female
cone

Huge numbers of conifers are felled to provide paper and building timber.

GRAND or GIANT FIR

(Abies grandis)

A native of the west coast of North America, this fast-growing tree is planted for its timber in northern and central Europe, where it grows to 54m.

Crown: narrow and conical, with the branches in regular whorls.

Bark: brown-grey, with resin blisters, becoming darker and cracked into small square plates with age.

Shoots: smooth and olive green.

Buds: purple, becoming coated with resin; 2mm long.

Leaves: soft needles with notched tips, shiny green above with two silver bands beneath; 2–5cm long. They are arranged in two rows along the twigs.

Cones: erect and cylindrical, 7–10cm long, maturing from light green to red-brown.

Uses: pale cream or white timber for boxes, paper pulp, etc.

19

mature female cone

Atlas Cedar

ATLAS CEDAR
(Cedrus atlanticus)

Outside its native Atlas Mountains in North Africa, this cedar is commonly planted as an ornamental tree in parks and gardens and is sometimes grown for timber in southern Europe; it reaches a height of 40m.

Crown: broad and conical; the branches grow up from the trunk and their tips turn upwards.

Bark: smooth and dark grey, becoming cracked and scaly with age.

Buds: light red-brown and egg-shaped with black-tipped scales; 2–3mm long.

Leaves: stiff green or bluish-green needles, 1–3cm long, growing in tufts of up to 45 on short spurs; they form flat plates of foliage on the branches.

Male cones: conical, 3–5cm long.

Female cones: erect and barrel-shaped, with a hollow at the tip, maturing in 2 years to a pale purple-brown colour; 5–8cm long. The fan-shaped scales fall off to release winged seeds, leaving a central axis on the tree.

Uses: pinkish fragrant fine-grained timber, durable and highly valued, used for cigar boxes, planking for yachts, lining clothes chests and cupboards, etc.

CEDAR OF LEBANON
(Cedrus libani)

A native of the eastern Mediterranean, from the Lebanon Mountains (in Syria and south-east Turkey, the cedar of Lebanon is widely planted as an ornamental tree in parks, gardens, and churchyards; grows to 40m. It is distinguished from the Atlas cedar by the following features:

Crown: conical, becoming flat-topped with wide-spreading level branches.

Leaves: dark grass-green needles, 2–3cm long, growing in tufts of 10 to 20 on short spurs.

Female cones: like the Atlas cedar but larger – 7–12cm long.

Cedar of Lebanon

mature female cone

DEODAR *(Cedrus deodara)*

The deodar forms forests in the western Himalayas, at a height of 2000–3000m. It is commonly planted as an ornamental tree and, in southern Europe, occasionally for its timber; it grows to 36m. It can be recognized by the following features:

Crown: conical, with spreading branches that droop down at the tips.

Shoots: pale brown, arched, and densely covered with hairs.

Buds: pointed, orange with pale-tipped scales; 1mm long.

Leaves: dark green needles, 2–5cm long, growing in tufts on short spurs.

Male cones: cylindrical, 5–12cm long.

Female cones: up to 14cm long, with rounded tips.

mature female cone

Deodar

EUROPEAN LARCH

(Larix decidua)

Native to central Europe – from the Alps to the West Carpathians – this graceful deciduous conifer is planted in northern and western Europe as an ornamental tree and for its strong, highly-prized timber; it grows to 40m.
Crown: narrow and conical, becoming flat-topped with age. The branches tend to droop down, then turn up at the tips.
Bark: grey-brown and smooth, splitting into vertical cracks with age.
Shoots: pale yellow or pale pink, long, and hanging down from the branches.
Buds: brown, scaly, and resinous.
Leaves: soft needles, 2–3cm long, growing in clusters of 20 to 30 from short spurs on the twigs. Emerald green in March, they become darker, and finally golden in autumn.

Male cones: small, round, and golden, 0·5–1cm long.
Female cones: pale to rose-red, and flower-like, 1cm long, maturing to brown, egg-shaped cones, 2–4cm by 2–3cm, with rounded scales.
Uses: strong durable resinous timber, with yellowish sapwood and red-brown heartwood, used for fencing, gates, planking for fishing boats, stair-

natural distribution of European larch

European Larch

winter

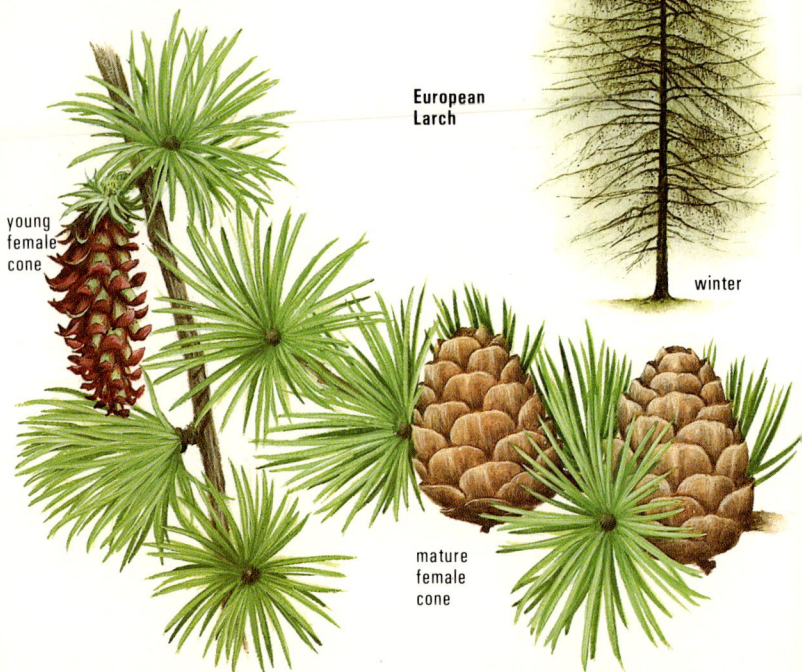

young female cone

mature female cone

22

cases, wall panelling, light furniture, telegraph poles, railway sleepers, pit-props, etc. The bark yields tannins used in tanning and dyeing; ethyl alcohol is distilled from the wood.

JAPANESE LARCH

(Larix kaempferi)

Because it is faster growing and more resistant to disease, this species is now often planted instead of the European larch. Native to the slopes of Mount Fuji and neighbouring peaks, the Japanese larch reaches a height of 35m.

Crown: broad and conical; the tips of the branches tend to turn upwards.
Bark: smooth and reddish-brown becoming scaly with age.
Shoots: dark orange-red, long, and hanging down from the branches.
Buds: reddish-brown and resinous.
Leaves: broader than those of the European larch, 3·5–4cm by 0·1cm; grey-green or blue-green, they fade to a rich orange before falling.
Male cones: like the European species but smaller.
Female cones: erect, cream or greenish, ripening to brown bun-shaped cones, 3 by 3cm, with the edges of the scales turned out and down towards the base of the cone.
Uses: see European larch.

NORWAY SPRUCE

(Picea abies)

A conifer of central and northern Europe, the Norway spruce is widely grown in forests, plantations, shelter belts, gardens, etc., for Christmas trees and timber; it grows to 40m.
Crown: narrow and conical; the branches are level except at the top, where they grow up from the trunk.
Bark: smooth and reddish-brown,

Japanese Larch

mature
female
cones

23

becoming dark purple with age and flaking into small rounded scales.

Shoots: reddish or orange-brown.

Buds: smooth, brown, and pointed.

Leaves: dark-green sharp-pointed four-sided needles, 1–2cm long, growing from pegs all round the twigs.

Male cones: globular and yellow, 1cm long, hanging down from the tips of the shoots.

Female cones: erect, oval, green or dark red; when fertilized they become dark brown and cylindrical, 12–18cm long, and hang down.

Uses: strong light elastic pale-yellow timber for boxes, interior joinery, barrels, paper pulp, chipboard, violin and cello bellies, etc. The wood fibres are woven into mats and screens. Turpentine is extracted from blisters on the trunk and branches.

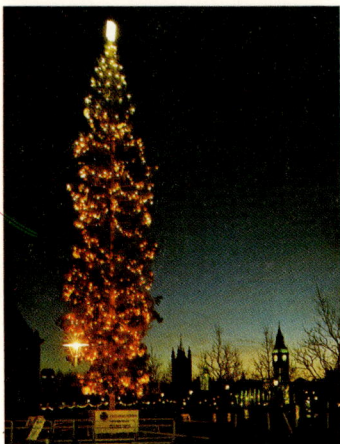

An illuminated Norway spruce used as a Christmas tree in London.

Norway Spruce

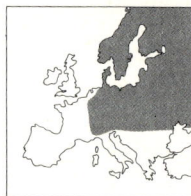

natural distribution of Norway spruce

male cones with pollen

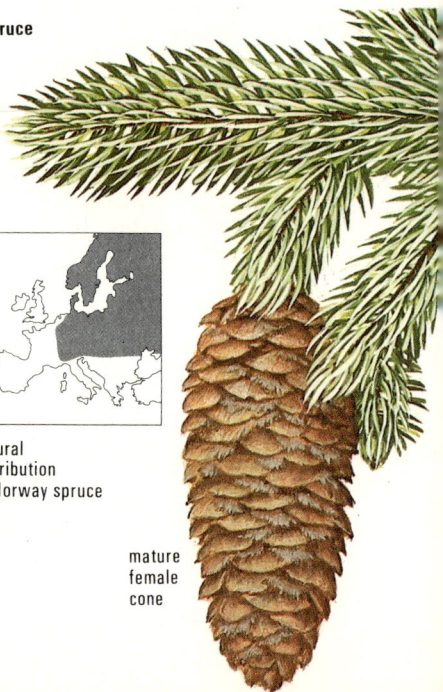

mature female cone

24

SITKA or SILVER SPRUCE *(Picea sitchensis)*

Native to the coastal regions of western North America, from Alaska to North California, this fast-growing spruce is now widely planted in northern, west, and central Europe for its useful timber; grows to 80m in North America, 50m in Europe. It can be recognized by the following features:

Crown: narrow and conical, with a long spire-like tip; in older trees the branches droop and the crown broadens.

Bark: dark grey or grey-brown and speckled; it flakes off in purplish scales in older trees.

Leaves: slender flat sharp-pointed needles, 1—3cm long, bluish-green above with two blue-white bands beneath.

Ripe female cones: light brown to whitish, blunt, and cylindrical, 5—10cm long; the scales are thin and papery with crinkled edges.

Uses: strong light fine-grained timber for interior joinery, boxes, carpentry, paper pulp, chipboard, pit-props, etc.

Sitka Spruce

mature female cones

Arolla Pine

mature female cone

needle cluster

AROLLA or SWISS STONE PINE

(Pinus cembra)

This pine occurs at an altitude of just under 3000m in the Alps and Carpathians (which is close to the limit for tree growth). It is planted in other parts of Europe for ornament and timber and grows to a height of 25m.
Crown: columnar; stout level branches with upturned tips grow right from the base of the trunk.
Bark: dark grey or orange-brown, becoming scaly and rugged with broad cracks.
Shoots: greenish-brown, densely covered with orange-brown down.
Leaves: needles, 7—9cm long, growing in dense bunches of five; their outer surface is shiny dark green, the inner surface green-white.
Cones: egg-shaped, 8 by 6cm, ripening from purple to shiny red-brown. The edible seeds are released after the cone has fallen and rotted.
Uses: the pale resinous timber, which is easily worked, is used for furniture, turned articles, and toys.

MONTEREY PINE

(Pinus radiata)

This wind-resistant tree, native to Monterey Bay in South California, is grown in mild coastal regions of western Europe for shelter and ornament; fast-growing, it is planted commercially in Spain, South Africa, Australia, and New Zealand. It grows to 30m.
Crown: conical, becoming broader and round-topped with age; branches grow low down on the trunk.
Bark: dark brown or dull grey, with deep cracks.
Buds: brownish, pointed, and covered with resin; 1—2cm long.
Leaves: slender bright-green needles,

growing in threes; 10—15cm long.
Cones: large and irregular — 7—14cm by 5—8cm and flattened on the side nearest to the stem — with glossy brown scales. These cones grow in clusters of 3 to 5 and remain on the tree for many years.
Uses: timber for boxes and paper pulp.

WEYMOUTH PINE
(Pinus strobus)

A native of eastern North America, the Weymouth pine is widely cultivated in central and western Europe for its timber; it grows to 30—40m.
Crown: narrow and conical, becoming irregular and flat-topped with age.
Bark: smooth and greenish-brown in young trees, becoming grey-black and cracked with age.
Shoots: slender and bright green, becoming greenish brown and covered with fine hairs.
Leaves: slender bluish-green needles, 8—12cm long, growing in bundles of

five, form horizontal masses on the branches.
Cones: brown and banana-shaped, 10—15cm long, hanging down from the stem; scales curve outwards. Young cones are green and straighter.
Uses: pale-brown, light, fine-textured timber for doors, window frames and general purposes.

bark of Weymouth pine

Monterey Pine

Weymouth Pine

mature female cone

mature female cone

AUSTRIAN PINE

(Pinus nigra var. *nigra)*

Native to Austria, central Italy, and the Balkans, this hardy wind-resistant pine is commonly planted on coasts as a wind-break and screen and to stabilize sand dunes; it grows to 33m.

Crown: irregular and spreading, with dark black-brown upper branches.

Bark: black-brown to dark grey, very scaly and coarsely ridged.

Shoots: shining yellow-brown, stout and ridged.

Buds: pale-brown and broad-based, 1cm long, tapering to a sharp point.

Leaves: stiff dark-green to black needles, curved and sharp-pointed, growing in pairs; 10–15cm long.

Cones: yellow- to grey-brown, egg-shaped and pointed; 5–8cm long.

CORSICAN PINE

(Pinus nigra var. *maritima)*

This fast-growing pine, native to Corsica, southern Italy, and Sicily, is planted for shelter and yields a useful timber; grows to 35m. It can be distinguished from the Austrian pine by the following features:

Crown: narrow and conical, with level branches.

Bark: pink-grey to dark brown, with shallow cracks.

Buds: 2cm long, with a long point.

Leaves: flexible grey-green or sage-green needles, often twisted, growing in pairs; 12–18cm long.

Uses: hard strong timber, with reddish heartwood surrounded by pale-brown sapwood, used for general construction work in the Mediterranean (see Scots pine for details); it also yields a useful resin.

Corsican Pine

Austrian Pine

mature female cone

28

SCOTS PINE

(Pinus sylvestris)

natural
distribution
of Scots pine

Native over much of Europe and northern and western Asia, the Scots pine is very widely planted for its valuable timber; it also makes an attractive hardy ornamental tree, thriving in light acid soils. Grows to 35—40m.

Crown: pyramid-shaped or conical when young, becoming flat-topped or rounded with age, with the branches sparsely arranged high up on the trunk.

Bark: at the base of the trunk reddish or grey-brown and cracked; on the upper trunk and branches orange-red to pink, and scaly.

Shoots: hairless and pale green, becoming brown.

Buds: cylindrical, dark brown or red.

Leaves: blue-grey or blue-green needles, often twisted, growing in pairs; 3—7cm long.

Male cones: small, yellow, and rounded, clustered near the tips of the shoots in early summer.

Female cones: pink and globular when fertilized, becoming green and turning down on the stem during the next year. Mature third-year cones, 3—8cm long, are grey-brown, oval, and pointed; they produce winged seeds.

Scots pine trees can be recognized by the orange-red bark on the upper parts of the trunk.

Scots Pine

mature
female
cone

Uses: yields a good multi-purpose resinous timber with reddish heartwood and pale-brown sapwood: one of the best softwoods for general construction, telegraph poles, railway sleepers, fencing, pit-props, paper pulp, chipboard, etc. Other products are pitch and tar; oil of turpentine and rosin (from the resin); and a reddish-yellow dye (from the cones).

ALEPPO PINE

(Pinus halepensis)

A Mediterranean species, the Aleppo pine is a familiar sight in hot dry coastal regions. It thrives on exposed limestone hills and rocky ground, checking soil erosion and acting as a wind-break, and has many important uses in the Mediterranean region; it grows to 20m.

Crown: narrow when young, becoming domed with age with twisting branches supported on a stout trunk.

Bark: purple- or reddish-brown, with deep cracks.

Shoots: pale and slender, greenish-brown or yellowish.

Buds: red-brown, cylindrical, 1cm long.

Leaves: long slender flexible bright-green needles, usually in pairs; 9–15cm long.

Cones: bright reddish-brown, pointed or egg-shaped, 5–12cm long; borne on short down-turned stalks, they remain on the tree for several years.

Uses: coarse-grained resinous timber for furniture, ships, houses, pitch, and fuel. The tree is also tapped for resin, which yields turpentine oil and is used for preserving wine; its bark is used for tanning skins.

STONE or UMBRELLA PINE

(Pinus pinea)

Native to the western Mediterranean, this wind-resistant pine has been planted in coastal regions all over the Mediterranean region since Roman times; it grows to 30m.

Crown: umbrella-shaped, with large spreading branches supported on a

short trunk: an unmistakable feature of the Mediterranean landscape.

Bark: red-brown or orange, deeply cracked and scaly.

Shoots: pale greyish-green and curved.

Buds: red-brown, with deeply fringed white scales that turn out.

Aleppo Pine

mature female cones

Left: An Aleppo pine trunk, cut so that resin will run into the pot at the bottom of the cut.

Leaves: dark greyish-green sharp-pointed needles, growing in pairs; 12—20cm long.
Cones: shining brown, globular, and flat-based, 10—15cm by 8—10cm; the scales are rounded and each has a central boss. The seeds are edible.
Uses: the rich oily seeds are eaten raw or roasted and used as a flavouring; the timber is used locally for furniture and general construction.

Stone Pine

mature
female cone

MARITIME PINE
(Pinus pinaster)

The maritime pine is native to the coasts of central and western Mediterranean regions; it grows best in light well-drained soils and is often planted for shelter and to reclaim sand dunes,

Maritime Pine

mature
female
cone

as well as for its timber; grows to 30m.
Crown: pyramid-shaped, with spreading branches growing high up on the trunk.
Bark: pale grey or reddish-brown with deep cracks, becoming darker with age.
Shoots: pinkish- or reddish-brown and hairless.
Buds: bright red-brown and non-resinous, with fringed scales.
Leaves: stout leathery sharp-pointed needles, growing in pairs; 15—25cm long.
Cones: bright glossy brown and pointed, up to 22cm long; the scales each have an upturned prickle. Cones remain on the branches for several years before opening.
Uses: tapped for resin, which yields turpentine oil (used in solvents for paints and varnishes) and rosin (used in paints, varnishes, soaps, and linoleum); timber used for general construction work, telegraph poles, pit-props, and paper pulp.

DOUGLAS FIR

(Pseudotsuga menziesii)

Native to western North America, this tall fast-growing tree is very widely planted in Europe for its timber. Growing to 100m in North America, it attains a height of 50m or more in Europe. It is not closely related to the true firs (p 18) and can be distinguished from them by its cones (see below).

Crown: pyramid-shaped, becoming flat-shaped with age.

Bark: dark grey and resin-blistered in young trees, becoming red-brown or purplish and corky, with deep cracks and ridges, with age.

Shoots: pale- or yellowish-green, covered with fine hairs.

Buds: pale brown and spindle-shaped, up to 7mm long; non-resinous.

Leaves: flexible aromatic needles, 2–3cm long, with two white bands underneath each side of the midrib; they grow singly on the stems and leave smooth oval scars when they fall.

Cones: dull brown and cylindrical, 5–8cm by 2·5cm, hanging down from the stem; the scales each have a three-lobed bract, which points towards the tip of the cone.

Uses: strong durable timber, with pinkish-brown heartwood and pale brown sapwood, for construction, flooring, joinery, fencing, pit-props, paper pulp, telegraph poles, and masts.

Douglas Fir

young
female
cones

male
cones

mature
female cone

A stand of Douglas fir trees showing the tall, straight trunks. The lowest branches have died through lack of light and have fallen.

32

WESTERN HEMLOCK *(Tsuga heterophylla)*

bark of Western hemlock

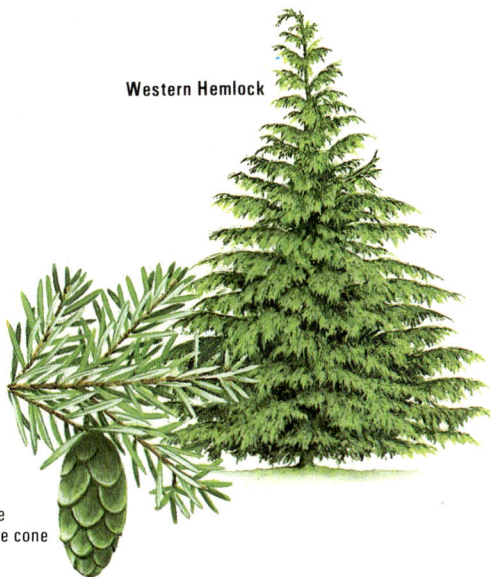

Western Hemlock

unripe
female cone

This graceful fast-growing conifer is native to the west coast of North America, where it may reach a height of 70m. A producer of good-quality timber, it is widely grown in north-west Europe; it prefers shade and is frequently planted under hardwood trees. It grows to 50m.

Crown: pyramid-shaped or conical, with a spire-like tip that arches over; the tips of the branches droop down.

Bark: brown, smooth, and flaky in young trees; becomes darker, with deep furrows and scaly ridges, with age.

Shoots: ribbed, pale yellow-brown, and covered with long hairs.

Buds: small, brown, and globular.

Leaves: flattened aromatic needles of different sizes 5–15mm long, with rounded tips; shining dark green above, they have two white bands along each side of the midrib on the lower surface. The needles have short stalks, and leave round orange scars on the twigs when they fall.

Cones: pale brown and egg-shaped, 2–3cm long, with smooth rounded scales; they hang down from the ends of the twigs. Unripe cones are green.

Uses: produces strong fine-textured pale-yellow timber with a darker heartwood, used for construction, joinery, boxes, paper pulp, etc.

EASTERN HEMLOCK
(Tsuga canadensis)

A native of eastern North America, this hemlock is similar to the western species but its timber is of inferior quality. It is often planted in Europe for ornament and occasionally for timber; it grows to 32m. It can be distinguished from the other species by the following features:

Crown: broad and conical.

Buds: egg-shaped; green with a brown tip.

Cones: small – 1·5–2cm.

SWAMP CYPRESS FAMILY *(Taxodiaceae)*

Most of the trees in this primitive family, which was once large and widely distributed, are now extinct. Those that remain – about 14 species – can be regarded as living fossils. They have awl-like or flattened needles and usually rounded, woody or leathery, cones.

JAPANESE RED CEDAR

(Cryptomeria japonica)

Native to China and Japan, this conifer is planted in parks and gardens in Europe as an ornamental tree and it is sometimes grown for its timber. Reaching a height of 50m in Japan, it grows to 37m in Europe.
Crown: narrow and conical, with a rounded top; the ends of the lower branches turn up.
Bark: thick, soft, and reddish-brown, with deep cracks; it peels off in long shreds.
Leaves: bright- or yellowish-green awl-shaped needles, up to 15mm long, growing all round the smaller branches the pointed tips of the needles curve forward.
Male cones: yellow and egg-shaped, 3mm across, growing in clusters near the tips of the branches.
Female cones: dark brown and globular, 2–3cm across, growing from the tips of the branches (which turn up); each cone scale bears a triangular flap that points towards the base of the cone and carries 3 to 5 erect spines.

DAWN REDWOOD

(Metasequoia glyptostroboides)

The first living specimen of recent times was discovered in south-west China in 1941; before this time the dawn redwood, or fossil tree, was regarded as an extinct species. Growing wild only in eastern Szechwan and north-east Hupeh, this deciduous conifer is now quite widely planted in parks and gardens of north-west Europe for ornament: its foliage assumes a range of attractive colours

Japanese
Red
Cedar

mature
female
cone

throughout the seasons. In the wild it grows to 35m, and some introduced trees have already reached a height of 19m.

Crown: conical, with branches that grow upward from the trunk.

Bark: pinkish-brown with reddish flakes, becoming darker and cracked with age and peeling off.

Leaves: thin soft flat needles, 2–4cm long, arranged in two rows along green deciduous branches, 10–12cm long. In spring the leaves are pale grey-green, later becoming bright green above and light green beneath; they change to pale pinkish-yellow in October, then to brick-red, and finally to deep rust-red in November.

Male cones: small and egg-shaped, 4mm long.

Female cones: green, globular or cylindrical, up to 2·5cm long; they hang down from stalks 5cm long. Introduced trees are more easily grown from cuttings than from seed.

COAST REDWOOD

(Sequoia sempervirens)

This majestic tree is native to western North America, its natural range being restricted to a narrow strip of coast from south-west Oregon to California. An important timber tree in North America, it is planted in Europe mainly for ornament in parks and gardens but occasionally for its timber. The redwood is considered to be the tallest tree in the world: a specimen of over 112m has been recorded in California; it grows to about 40m in Europe. It is also one of the longest lived: some Californian trees are over 2000 years old.

Crown: columnar, with level or drooping branches; the trunk is often buttressed at its base.

Bark: rusty red, soft, and fibrous, becoming darker, thicker, and deeply cracked with age.

Dawn Redwood

Coast Redwood

autumn leaves

young female cones

Coast Redwood

mature
female cone

leaves on the main stems of the branches are smaller and awl-shaped.
Male cones: small, rounded, and yellowish, in clusters at the tips of the main shoots.
Female cones: woody and globular, 2–2·5cm long, with wrinkled red-brown scales attached to the centre of the cone. They produce winged seeds.
Uses: soft strong durable timber, with pale-yellow sapwood and red-brown heartwood, suitable for garden furniture, fencing, etc., as well as for cabinet work.

Shoots: green and hairless, surrounded by green scale leaves.
Buds: short and scaly.
Leaves: hard, flattened, and blade-like, 1·5–2cm long, dark green above with a white band along each side of the midrib beneath; arranged in two rows along the side-branches. The

Left: Coast redwoods are the tallest trees in the world, reaching heights of more than 100 metres.
Below: The enormous trunks of the giant sequoia or 'big tree'. The bark is very soft and can be punched without hurting one's fist.

GIANT SEQUOIA

(Sequoiadendron giganteum)

The most massive – but not the tallest – tree in the world, the giant sequoia forms natural forests in California's Sierra Nevada, where it grows to over 80m, with a girth of 24m, and lives for over 3000 years. In Europe it is planted for ornament, reaching a height of 50m and a girth of 7m.
Crown: narrow and conical; the ends of the branches curve upwards.
Bark: reddish-brown, thick, soft, and fibrous; becomes darker, fluted, and deeply cracked with age.

Leaves: blue-green or dark-green pointed scales, 4–7mm long, densely covering the branchlets.

Cones: brown and egg-shaped, 5–8cm long, drooping down from stalks at the ends of the branches; the scales are attached at the centre.

Uses: the soft strong durable reddish-brown timber of North American trees is used for planking, posts, and garden furniture; the timber of European trees is less durable.

Giant Sequoia or Wellingtonia or Big Tree

mature female cone

CYPRESS FAMILY *(Cupressaceae)*

The hundred or more species of evergreens in this family are found in the cooler regions of both hemispheres and on mountain tops in the tropics and subtropics. They often have two kinds of leaves – needle-like juvenile leaves and scalelike adult leaves – and small woody cones (except the junipers, which have fleshy cones).

LAWSON CYPRESS *(Chamaecyparis lawsoniana)*

A tree of western North America — from north-west California and south-west Oregon — Lawson cypress is very widely planted in northern and central Europe for shelter and ornament. Many cultivated varieties are seen in parks, gardens, and churchyards; the tree is also planted commercially for timber on a small scale. Growing to 60m in America, it reaches a height of 38m in Europe.

Crown: narrow and conical; the tips of the branches droop down.

Bark: smooth, grey-brown, and shiny, becoming purplish-brown, cracked, and flaking off in older trees.

Leaves: bright green, triangular, and scale-like, borne on flattened branched twigs in horizontal sprays, like fern fronds. There are also cultivated varieties with golden and blue-green foliage.

Male cones: crimson and club-shaped, 5mm long, at the tips of the branches.

Female cones: green and globular, borne at the tips of the shorter branches, ripening to woody purple-brown cones, 7–8mm in diameter, producing winged seeds.

Uses: produces strong light durable timber, with yellow-white sapwood and dark-brown heartwood, for joinery, fencing, and underwater construction.

Lawson Cypress

mature
female
cone

young
female cone

*Several varieties
of Lawson
cypress growing
in a landscaped
garden.*

LEYLAND CYPRESS
(Cupressocyparis leylandii)

This hybrid was first produced in 1858, by C. J. Leyland, using the Nootka cypress *(Chamaecyparis nootkatensis)* and the Monterey cypress (see p 40) as parent species. Since then several hardy, fast-growing varieties have been raised and the tree is now widely planted in parks and gardens in north-west Europe. Growing to 30m, it is usually propagated by cuttings.

Crown: columnar, tapering to a pointed tip.

Bark: dark red-brown, with shallow cracks.

Leaves: scale-like, of various colours (dark grey-green to blue-green, depending on the variety), clothing branched sprayed twigs.

Male cones: brown and club-shaped, at the tips of the branches.

Female cones: globular and greenish, ripening to grey or chocolate-brown cones, up to 1·5cm in diameter.

Leyland
Cypress

MONTEREY CYPRESS
(Cupressus macrocarpa)

Native to California, the Monterey cypress — quick-growing and salt-resistant — is planted in western and southern Europe both for shelter and ornament in parks, gardens, church-yards and by the sea, and also for its timber. It reaches a height of 37m.
Crown: columnar, with a pointed top, becoming spreading and flat-topped with age.
Bark: brown with shallow ridges, becoming grey with thick peeling ridges in very old trees.
Leaves: scale-like and blunt-tipped, bright- or dark-green with paler margins; 1—2mm long. They completely cover the twigs and smell of lemon when crushed.
Male cones: yellow and egg-shaped, 3mm long, borne on small side-shoots.
Female cones: egg-shaped, green and purple, 6mm long, on central shoots; they ripen to rounded lumpy cones, 3—4cm long, with shining purple-brown scales each with a central boss.

Mexican Cypress

mature
female
cone

MEXICAN CYPRESS
(Cupressus lusitanica)

The Mexican cypress is occasionally planted for ornament in Europe, most commonly in the south; it reaches a height of 30m.

Monterey Cypress

unripe
female
cone

40

Crown: conical, becoming flat-topped with age.

Bark: brown, peeling off in vertical strips.

Leaves: dark green and scale-like, with pointed spreading tips; they smell faintly of resin when crushed.

Female cones: globular, 1·5cm across, with a central point on each cone scale; blue-grey at first, the cones ripen to a shining deep purple-brown colour.

Italian Cypress

ITALIAN or
FUNERAL CYPRESS

(Cupressus sempervirens)

This handsome Mediterranean cypress is commonly planted in gardens and cemeteries, especially in the Mediterranean region; it also yields a highly valued timber. The tree grows to 23m.

Crown: usually narrow and columnar, tapering to a pointed tip, but may be pyramid-shaped, with spreading level branches.

unripe
female
cone

Bark: brown-grey, with shallow spiralled ridges.

Leaves: dark green, scale-like, and triangular, 1mm long, arranged in overlapping rows that completely cover the twigs.

Male cones: greenish and egg-shaped, 3mm long, at the tips of the twigs.

Female cones: greenish and globular, becoming dark red-brown and finally dull grey, 4 by 3cm; the scales each have a central spine.

Uses: strong durable fragrant timber, resistant to decay, used for carving, furniture, stakes, and vine props. The crushed leaves and seeds have medicinal properties.

The tall, slender Italian cypress gives a regal appearance to many formal gardens. It is often planted in cemeteries, hence its alternative name of funeral cypress. The yellow flowers in the foreground of the photograph are those of the Spanish broom.

41

COMMON JUNIPER
(Juniperus communis)

Very widely distributed in the northern hemisphere — from North America to south-west Asia and from Siberia to the Mediterranean — this adaptable small tree or shrub grows well on poor soils in a variety of habitats; it reaches a height of 6m.
Crown: variable – usually pointed but may be wide-spreading and broad.
Bark: reddish-brown.
Leaves: sharp-pointed needles, 1cm long, spreading out from the stems in whorls of three; there is a whitish band on the upper surface and the lower surface is grey-green.
Male and female cones grow on separate trees, in the axils of the needles.
Male cones: solitary, yellow, and cylindrical; 4mm long.
Female cones: greenish and globular, ripening in 2 to 3 years to blue-black berry-like fruits, 6–9mm in diameter.
Uses: the ripe berries are used for

male cones

Chinese Juniper

Common Juniper

mature, berry-like female cones

CHINESE JUNIPER
(Juniperus chinensis)

Native to China and Japan, this juniper is very widely planted for ornament in parks and gardens; it reaches a height of 18m.
Crown: narrow and conical, often becoming broader and many-stemmed with age.
Bark: dark brown, peeling off in long twisted strips.
Leaves: tufts of needles (juvenile leaves), grey-blue on the inner side, grow at the bases of the branchlets; blunt scale (adult) leaves, dull dark green with paler margins, densely cover the shoots. Cultivated varieties may have golden or blue-green leaves. Male and female cones grow on separate trees.
Male cones: small and yellow, growing at the tips of the branchlets throughout winter.
Female cones: rounded, bluish-white, and berry-like, 6–7mm across, ripening in 2 years.

42

flavouring gin and seasoning food; oil of juniper is distilled from the unripe fruits. Cultivated varieties of juniper are often grown in gardens as small ornamental trees. The wood is durable and of high quality, but too little is produced to be of any economic importance.

CADE or PRICKLY JUNIPER
(Juniperus oxycedrus)

The prickly juniper is widespread in its native Mediterranean region, growing in coastal parts, dry hills, rocky ground, and woods; it reaches a height of 8m.
Crown: basically conical and densely branched.
Leaves: sharp-pointed or blunt needles, 16mm long, with two white bands along either side of the midrib on the upper surface.
Female cones: (on separate trees from the males): rounded and berry-like, ripening from green to reddish or yellowish; 6–10mm in diameter.

Pencil Cedar

mature female cone

Prickly Juniper

mature female cones

Uses: oil of cade, used in medicine and veterinary work, is distilled from the wood; the wood is very resistant to decay and is used for making charcoal.

PENCIL CEDAR
(Juniperus virginiana)

An important timber tree in its native North America, the pencil cedar is sometimes grown for timber in south and central Europe; it reaches a height of 30m. Elsewhere in Europe, it is widely planted as an ornamental tree (up to 15m tall).
Crown: conical, becoming broad and spreading with age.
Bark: reddish-brown and peeling.
Leaves: needles (juvenile leaves) grow at the tips of the shoots; pointed scale leaves clothe the branchlets.
Female cones (on separate trees from the males): rounded and berry-like ripening in one year.
Uses: the durable easily worked wood is used for pencils, chests, etc.

WHITE CEDAR
(Thuja occidentalis)

White Cedar

Western Red Cedar

mature female cone

mature female cone

White Cedar

Unrelated to the true cedars (see p 20), this conifer from eastern North America is quite widely planted in Europe in many cultivated forms as an ornamental; it grows to 20m.

Crown: narrow and conical, with a rounded top and upswept branches; becomes irregular in older trees.

Bark: orange-brown, thick, and fibrous, with vertical ridges.

Leaves: scale-like and pointed, growing in sprays on flattened twigs; the underside is pale yellowish, the upper surface yellow-green or dark green.

Cones: yellow and urn-shaped, 8mm long, made up of 8 to 10 scales.

WESTERN RED CEDAR
(Thuja plicata)

An important timber tree of western North America, the western red cedar is cultivated in parks, gardens, and plantations in Europe for shelter and timber. Noted for its quick growth, it reaches a height of 40m.

Crown: narrow and conical, with a spire-like tip and upswept branches; it broadens with age.

Bark: reddish-brown and fibrous, becoming grey-brown and peeling off in strips.

Leaves: blunt and scale-like, growing in sprays on flattened twigs; the upper surface is bright glossy green, the undersurface paler with white streaks.

Male cones: yellow and very small, at the tips of the smallest shoots.

Female cones: leathery and egg-shaped, ripening from green to brown, 1·5cm long; they are each made up of 10 to 12 thin overlapping spreading spine-tipped scales and are borne at the tips of the branches.

Uses: soft light durable timber, with pale-yellow sapwood and orange-brown heartwood, used for joinery, outdoor construction, poles, fencing, etc.

**Western
Red
Cedar**

YEW FAMILY
(Taxaceae)

YEW *(Taxus baccata)*

Widely distributed in Europe, North Africa, and south-west Asia, the yew is commonly planted in many cultivated varieties in parks, gardens, and churchyards. Yews can live to a great age — it is estimated that some are over a thousand years old — and reach a height of 25m; their bark, shoots, leaves, and seeds are all poisonous.

Crown: rounded or pyramid-shaped and densely branched; the branches are level or upturned.

Bark: reddish-brown and flaking; becomes deeply furrowed with age.

Leaves: leathery, sharp-pointed needles, 1—4cm by 3 mm, very dark green above and yellowish-green underneath. They are arranged in two rows along the side branches.

Yew

bark of yew

mature
berry-like
female
cones

45

Male and female cones grow on separate trees in the axils of the leaves.
Male cones: small, rounded, and yellow, with overlapping scales.
Female cones: bright red and berry-like, enclosing a single seed; 1cm long.
Uses: the wood is hard, heavy, durable, strong, and elastic; in the Middle Ages it was used for bows, and more recently for cabinetwork, wood sculpture, etc.

Monkey Puzzle

female cone

MONKEY-PUZZLE FAMILY

(Araucariaceae)

spiky leaves

MONKEY PUZZLE

(Araucaria araucana)

The monkey puzzle — a native of Chile, Argentina, and as far south as Tierra del Fuego — is quite widely planted in Europe as an ornamental tree for its curious branching system. It can grow to 30m but cultivated trees are usually smaller.
Crown: broad and rounded; the stout branches grow in regular tiers, drooping down at the base of the tree, and all have up-turned ends.
Bark: smooth and grey.
Leaves: leathery, green, and triangular, 3—4cm long, each with a spiny tip; they overlap each other and completely cover the twigs and branches. Male and female cones usually grow on separate trees.
Male cones: dark brown and egg-shaped, 10—12cm long.
Female cones: nearly spherical, 15cm across, green with golden spines; they break up into scales on the tree. The large brown seeds are edible and usually eaten roasted.

46

PALM FAMILY
(Palmae)

This family of flowering plants is widespread in the tropics, and some palms are cultivated in subtropical and warm regions. Unlike broad-leaved trees, palms do not produce true wood, and their stems – which are unbranched – are covered with a layer of strong tough fibres, rather than bark. Palm stems are crowned by a tuft of leaves. In the feather palms each leaf consists of a row of leaflets along each side of the midrib; in fan palms the leaflets arise from the same point at the top of the leaf stalk.

Chusan palm (left) and canary palms growing on the Mediterranean coast.

CANARY PALM
(Phoenix canariensis)

This feather palm is native to the Canary Islands and is frequently planted as an ornamental in Mediterranean streets. It is related to the date palm but its fruit is inedible.
The slender stem is covered with old leaf bases and surmounted by a crown of glossy green leaves, each made up of pairs of long thin leaflets; the tree grows to 6–8m.
Flowers: small and yellowish, grouped together in large clusters.
Fruit: small and dry; 1·5cm across.

CHUSAN PALM
(Trachycarpus excelsus)

Native to south China and Japan, this tall fan palm is often grown as an ornamental both in the Mediterranean and also in warm regions elsewhere. The stout shaggy stem is covered with a mass of hard brown fibres and the woody bases of shed leaves; the tree reaches a height of 11m.
Leaves: rounded, each made up of 50–60 long narrow pointed leaflets. Borne on spiny leaf stalks, the leaves are a rich dark green, turning bright

Chusan
Palm

yellow and then dull brown before falling.

Flowers: yellow and very small, growing in drooping clusters, 60cm long; male and female flowers are usually in separate clusters.

Fruit: blue-black and globular; 1—1·5cm across.

DWARF FAN PALM

(Chamaerops humilis)

The only native European palm, the dwarf fan palm is found in dry regions along the Mediterranean coast — from Italy westwards but excluding France. It is widely cultivated; most forms are stemless but some have stout, fibre-covered trunks and may reach a height of 6—7m.

Leaves: rounded, each made up of 12 to 15 stiff pointed leaflets and borne on a slender spiny leaf stalk.

Flowers: small and yellow, in dense clusters that are at first sheathed in red spathes.

Fruit: brownish-yellow and globular; 2cm across.

The dwarf fan palm, with the trunk covered by fibrous old leaf bases.

Dwarf Fan Palm
with flower clusters

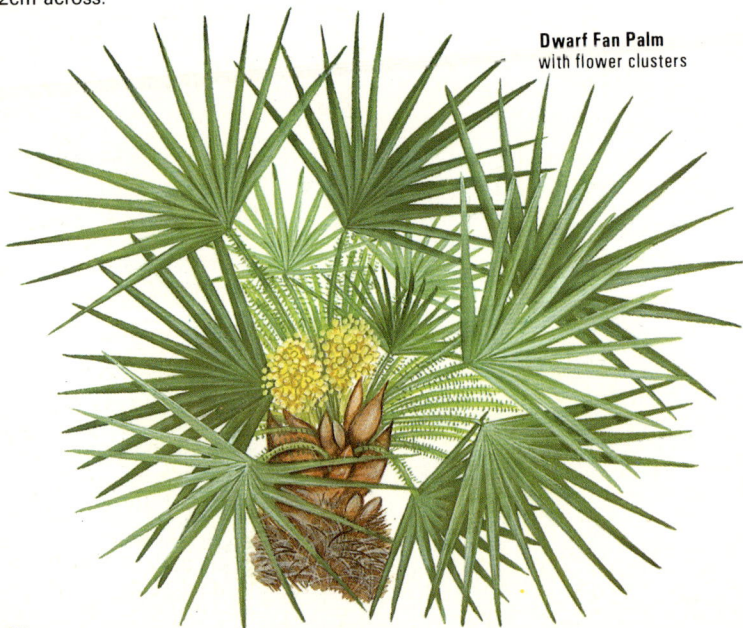

WILLOW FAMILY *(Salicaceae)*

The willows and poplars constitute nearly all the 300 or more species of deciduous trees and shrubs that make up this family. They all have flowers grouped into single-sexed catkins. The dry fruit – a capsule – splits to release seeds, which are covered in silky hairs.

winter

White Poplar

underside of leaf

ripe male catkins

ripe female catkins

WHITE POPLAR
(Populus alba)

Native to central and southern Europe and central and western Asia, the white poplar is widely planted as an ornamental in parks and gardens; it grows to 30m.

Crown: broadest at the top, with twisted spreading branches.

Bark: smooth and grey-white in young trees, becoming black and rough at the base and patchy above.

Shoots and buds: densely covered with white woolly down.

Leaves: either large (9 by 8cm) and 5-lobed or small (5 by 5cm) and usually oval, with toothed or lobed margins; all have stalks 3–4cm long. The undersurface and stalks are white and downy.

Male and female flowers (catkins), 4–8cm long, grow on separate trees.

Male catkins: crimson and grey.

Female catkins: pale green or greenish yellow, producing fluffy seeds.

49

BLACK POPLAR
(Populus nigra)

Widely distributed over much of Europe, this poplar is often planted as an ornamental tree; it grows to 35m and there are many varieties and hybrids.
Crown: broad, with upturned branches; the trunk is short and thick and often carries large burrs.
Bark: grey-brown to black, deeply furrowed into broad ridges.
Leaves: triangular to diamond-shaped, 5–8cm by 6–8cm, with translucent toothed margins; borne on 3–4cm-stalks, they are deep green above and paler beneath, turning a soft yellow. Male and female flowers (catkins) grow on separate trees.
Male catkins: grey, becoming crimson; 5cm long.
Female catkins: greenish-white, 6–7cm long, producing white woolly seeds.
Uses: soft light nearly white wood used for packing cases and general purposes.

bark of black poplar

LOMBARDY POPLAR
(Populus nigra var. italica)

This variety of the black poplar, produced in Italy, is now very widely planted for shade and ornament; it grows to 36m.
Crown: narrow and columnar, with a

Lombardy Poplar

ripe-female catkins

Aspen

underside of leaf

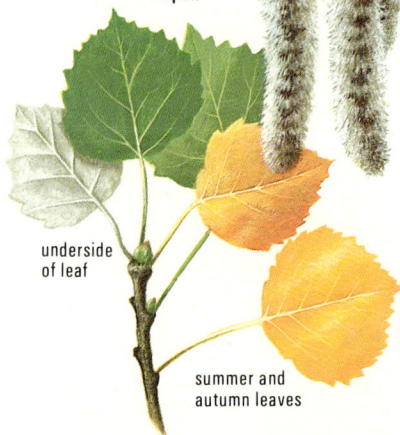

summer and autumn leaves

pointed tip and upswept branches.
Leaves: triangular, with a rounded base and small curved teeth; 6 by 4·5cm. Bright green, they are borne on flattened stalks, 2·5cm long.

ASPEN *(Populus tremula)*

Very widely distributed over the whole of Europe — and extending into the Arctic Circle — the aspen is most commonly found on hillsides and in damp places; it grows to 25m.
Crown: conical and sparsely branched, becoming broader with age.
Bark: greenish-grey and smooth, becoming brown and ridged at the base.
Buds: red-brown, sticky, and pointed.
Leaves: rounded, with curved irregular teeth; 4—6cm by 5—7cm. Borne on slender flattened stalks, 4—6cm long, they are dull rich green above and pale grey-green beneath.
Male and female flowers (catkins) grow on separate trees.
Male catkins: purplish-grey and downy, becoming yellow with pollen.
Female catkins: green, 4cm long, becoming woolly and white when they shed their seeds.
Uses: soft light white wood excellent for matches and paper pulp.

WHITE WILLOW

(Salix alba)

This willow is widely distributed in Europe, central Asia, and North Africa, often found growing by streams and rivers; it reaches a height of 25m.
Crown: conical, becoming rather shapeless with spreading branches.
Bark: dark grey with thick ridges.
Shoots: greyish-pink to olive-brown, slender, and hairy.
Buds: dark pinkish, covered with grey hairs.
Leaves: narrow and pointed, 7—8cm long, with toothed margins; blue-grey and covered with silky hairs.
Male and female flowers (catkins), 4—6cm long, grow on separate trees.
Male catkins: yellow, with 2 stamens to each flower.
Female catkins: green and slender, becoming white and fluffy with seed.

ripe
female
catkin

White Willow

natural
distribution
of white willow

Uses: light tough timber for flooring, cart bottoms, etc.; the pliant young twigs are used for basketry.

WEEPING WILLOW

(Salix vitellina var. *pendula; Salix x chrysocoma)*

One of several types of weeping willow, this hybrid is widely planted as an ornamental tree in parks, gardens, and by rivers; it grows to 22m.
Crown: broad and domed; the curved branches bear long slender yellow shoots that hang straight down.
Bark: pale grey-brown, with a network of shallow ridges.
Leaves: narrow and pointed, 10cm long; pale green above, bluish-white beneath, and covered with fine hairs.

SALLOW, GOAT WILLOW

(Salix capraea)

Native from Europe to north-east Asia, the sallow is common in damp wooded regions and coppices; it grows to 16m.

Crown: open, with upswept branches.
Bark: smooth and grey in young trees, becoming brown with wide cracks.
Shoots: deep red-brown and initially covered with long hairs.
Buds: red, oval, and pointed; 3–4mm.
Leaves: usually oval with a pointed tip and wavy margins; 10 by 6cm. Dark grey-green above and grey and woolly beneath, they have dark red hairy stalks with 2 small leaves at the base.

Male and female flowers (catkins) grow on separate trees and appear long before the leaves.

Male catkins: egg-shaped, 3cm long, and covered with silvery hairs; later they sprout golden-tipped stamens.
Female catkins: arched, slender (5–6cm long), and pale green with whitish styles, producing fluffy seeds.

Goat Willow

female catkins

male catkins with pollen

CRACK WILLOW

(Salix fragilis)

Found all over Europe and as far east as western Siberia and Persia, the crack willow is common in damp places, e.g. by rivers; it grows to 25m.
Crown: broad and conical with upswept branches, becoming domed with twisted branches.
Bark: grey and scaly, developing thick brownish ridges with age.
Shoots: greenish-brown, snapping off cleanly and readily at the base.
Buds: brown, slender, and pointed.
Leaves: narrow and pointed, 12cm long, bright green and glossy above, grey-green and waxy beneath.

Male and female flowers (catkins) grow on separate trees and appear with the leaves; they are slender, cylindrical, and pointed.
Male catkins: yellow; 2–5cm long.
Female catkins: green, 10cm long, becoming white and fluffy with seed.
Uses: hybrids between this species and the white willow are very common. The wood of one of these, *Salix x coerulea*, is used for cricket bats.

Crack Willow

female catkins

WALNUT FAMILY *(Juglandaceae)*

WALNUT *(Juglans regia)*

Thought to be native to south-west Europe and south-west Asia, the walnut is now naturalized in many parts of Europe; it grows to 30m.

Crown: rounded or spreading.

Bark: very pale grey, becoming deeply furrowed with age.

Buds: broad and squat; deep purple-brown to black.

Leaves: compound, with 3 to 4 leaflets down each side of the stalk and one (the largest) at the tip. Each leaflet is leathery and oval with a pointed tip, 8–20 by 4–10cm, and aromatic when crushed. Orange-brown when they first open, they become dull green above and paler beneath.

Male flowers: greenish-purple catkins, 5–10cm long, in the leaf axils.

Female flowers: greenish-yellow, 1cm long, in erect clusters of 2 to 5 at the tips of the shoots. They develop into globular dark-green fruits (drupes), the outer layer decaying to reveal the stone within.

Uses: the seeds are edible and yield a useful oil; the unripe fruits are pickled. A fast brown dye is obtained from the fruits and other parts. Walnut timber is hard, heavy, and fine-grained, with a pale grey-brown sapwood and chocolate-brown heartwood, and is attractively figured; it is highly valued for furniture, gunstocks, etc.

fruit opening to reveal stone

stone

section through stone

seed

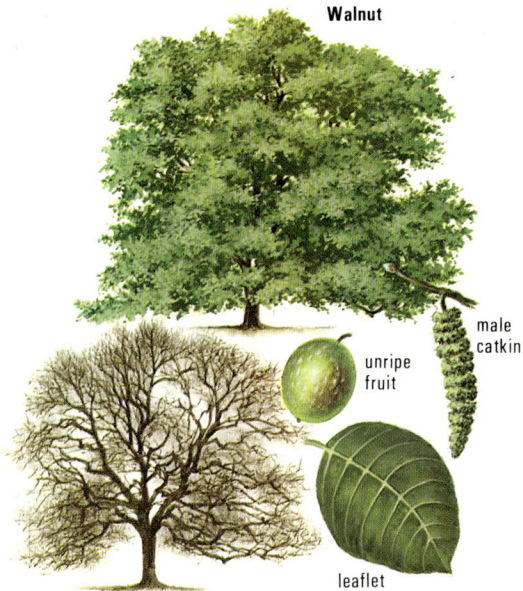
Walnut

male catkin

unripe fruit

leaflet

BIRCH FAMILY *(Betulaceae)*

The deciduous trees and shrubs of this
family – about 120 species – grow in
northern temperate regions. Their flowers
are grouped into separate male and female
inflorescences on the same tree: the males
are in long drooping catkins; the females in
shorter catkins or erect clusters. Some
authorities place the hornbeams and
hazels in a separate family – *Corylaceae*.

SILVER BIRCH
(Betula pendula)

This graceful slender tree, native to
most of Europe and south-west Asia,
grows well on light peaty sandy soils;
it reaches a height of 30m.

Crown: narrow and conical with
upswept branches, becoming rounded,
with long hanging branchlets and a
deeply fluted trunk.

Bark: shiny purplish-brown in young
trees, becoming pinkish-white and
finally white with black diamond-
shaped markings, smooth and peeling
above, black and knobbly at the base.

Shoots: dark purple-brown, with
raised white warts.

Leaves: emerald green and triangular,
with rounded bases and double-
toothed margins; 3–7cm long.

Male flowers: clusters of 2 to 4
drooping yellow catkins, 3cm long, at
the tips of the shoots; young catkins
are pale purple-brown and visible all
winter.

Female flowers: clusters of about 6
catkins on branched stalks below the
males; at first erect, green, and club-
shaped, 1–1·5cm long, they become
brown and hang down, 2–3cm long,
and release small winged fruits.

Uses: the hard strong pale-brown
wood is used for small turned articles
and, in Scandinavia, for plywood,
flooring, and skis; the twigs are used
for brooms and brushes and the bark
for roofing, tanning, etc.

Silver
Birch

winter

young
female
catkin

male
catkin

developing
female catkins

winged fruit

ripe
female
catkin.

autumn
leaf

COMMON ALDER
(Alnus glutinosa)

Found all over Europe and also in Siberia and North Africa, the common alder grows by open water — from mountain streams to lowland fens; it reaches a height of 25m.

Crown: broad and conical or pyramid-shaped; the spreading branches are at first unswept and later level.

Bark: purplish-brown, becoming dark grey-brown and cracked into small square plates.

Shoots: green and sticky, becoming purple with orange markings.

Buds: green to purple, 7mm long, borne on short stalks, 3mm long.

Leaves: oval, with a pointed base, a rounded tip, and wavy or toothed margins; 10 by 7cm. Pale orange-brown when they first open, they become very dark green.

Male and female flowers (catkins) appear before the leaves.

Male catkins: in clusters of 3 to 5, maturing from dull purple to dark yellow; 5cm long.

Female catkins: present all the year round in short erect clusters; dark red catkins, 5—6mm long, mature into

A common alder tree growing in its typical stream-side habitat.

developing male catkins

developing female catkins

young female catkins

fruit

old female catkins

mature male catkins

Common Alder

young
female
catkins

mature
male
catkins

mature
female
catkin

Grey Alder

developing
female
catkins

developing
male catkins

green egg-shaped cones, 8–15mm long, which become dark brown and woody when ripe.

Uses: the wood is strong, easily worked, and durable under water; it is used for piles, barrels, toys, broom-heads, hat blocks, etc., and paper pulp. This alder is often planted to conserve river and lake banks; it also improves the fertility of the soil.

GREY ALDER

(Alnus incana)

A tree of northern and central Europe, introduced into Britain, the grey alder flourishes in dry areas; because it grows rapidly on difficult soils, it is often planted in land reclamation schemes. It grows to 25m.

Crown: conical, becoming broad with age.

Bark: deep greenish-grey, smooth, and flaky, becoming dull dark grey and deeply cracked.

Shoots: red-brown above and olive beneath, with orange markings, covered with short grey hairs. Older shoots are pale shiny grey.

Buds: purple-red and curved, 8mm long, borne on stalks 2mm long.

Leaves: round or oval with a pointed tip and sharply toothed margins; up to 10 by 10cm. Dull green above and greyish beneath, they are covered with short hairs.

Male catkins: in clusters of 3 to 4, each 5–10cm long.

Female catkins: in clusters of 3 to 8 on pale brown downy stalks; they ripen to egg-shaped cones, 1 by 0·8cm.

bark of grey alder

HORNBEAM
(Carpinus betulus)

The natural range of this slow-growing wind-resistant tree is from the Pyrenees to southern Sweden and east as far as south-west Asia. It makes excellent hedges and produces hard timber; it grows to 30m.

Crown: rounded, with upswept branches and a deeply fluted trunk.

Bark: smooth and pale grey, sometimes with fine pale-brown stripes.

Buds: pale brown, slender, pointed, and turned in towards the stem.

Leaves: oval and pointed, with reddish stalks, double-toothed margins, and about 15 pairs of prominent parallel veins; 8–10 by 5–6·5cm. Very dark green above and yellowish beneath, they turn old gold in autumn.

Male flowers: bright yellow-green drooping catkins, 2·5–5cm long.

Female flowers: shorter catkins, made up of green leafy bracts each carrying two crimson-styled flowers. They develop into clusters of 3-lobed bracts, each 3·5cm long and bearing a pair of small nutlets.

Uses: tough heavy nearly white wood used for chopping blocks, mallets, skittles, wooden rollers, etc.

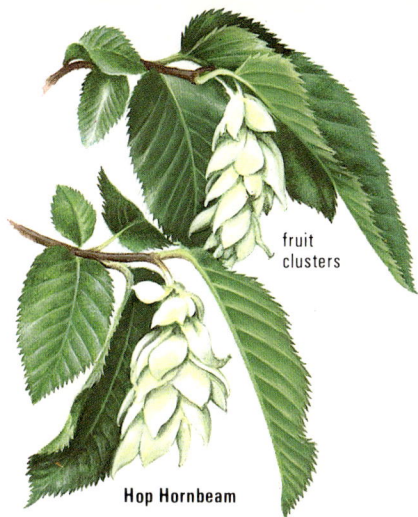

fruit clusters

Hop Hornbeam

Shoots: reddish-brown and hairy.

Buds: green and spindle-shaped.

Leaves: like the hornbeam but with sharper teeth; 5–12 by 3–6cm.

Fruit: clusters of about 15 white or greenish papery bladders, each 1·5–2cm long and enclosing a nutlet.

HOP HORNBEAM
(Ostrya carpinifolia)

Native to south Europe and southwest Asia, the hop hornbeam can be easily distinguished from the hornbeam by its fruit; it grows to 20m.

Bark: brown, with vertical cracks.

bark of hornbeam

male catkin

Hornbeam

fruit

winter twig

57

HAZEL *(Corylus avellana)*

Widely distributed in Europe and south-west Asia, the hazel is found in woods, thickets, and hedgerows; it can grow to 12m but is usually shorter (6m).

Crown: usually a broad bush, sometimes with a short trunk.

Bark: smooth and shiny grey-brown, with horizontal rows of pores.

Shoots: pale-brown, covered with long swollen-tipped (glandular) hairs.

Buds: smooth, blunt, and egg-shaped, changing from brown to green.

Leaves: rounded with a pointed tip and double-toothed margins, up to 10 by 10cm, borne on hairy stalks. Hairy and deep green above, they turn brown and finally yellow.

Male flowers: brownish-yellow catkins that appear in autumn, becoming yellow and longer (5cm) by spring.

Female flowers and fruit: small brown buds with protruding crimson stigmas develop into clusters of 1 to 4 nuts, each partly enclosed in a toothed green husk; the nuts change from whitish-green to pale pink-brown and finally brown by autumn.

Uses: the nuts are edible; the strong tough flexible mid-brown wood is used for hurdles, pea- and beansticks, hoops, etc., and formerly for wattle and daub building.

A hazel coppice. The trees were cut down to ground level about 10 years earlier and then each sent up several sturdy shoots or 'poles'.

BEECH FAMILY *(Fagaceae)*

This large and commercially important family – containing 800 to 1000 species of deciduous or evergreen trees and shrubs – is widely distributed in all temperate regions of the world. Flowers are borne in catkins and the fruit is a nut, partly or completely enclosed in a cuplike husk.

SWEET or SPANISH CHESTNUT *(Castanea sativa)*

This Mediterranean tree is widely grown for its edible nuts – it should not be confused with the horse chestnut whose nuts (conkers) are inedible. Long-lived and fast-growing, it does best on dry sandy soils; it reaches a height of over 30m.

Crown: conical and open when young, becoming columnar, and finally rounded and spreading.

Bark: silvery-green, becoming dark with deep, spirally arranged, cracks.

Shoots: stout and shiny purple-brown; smooth or downy.

Buds: rounded, yellow-green to red-brown.

Leaves: oblong, with a pointed tip and prominent parallel veins each extending into a bristly tooth on the margin; 10–25 by 9–10cm. Borne on red or yellowish stalks, 2·5cm long, they turn from bronze to glossy dark green, and finally pale yellow or rich brown in autumn.

Male and female flowers grow together in yellow spike-like catkins, 10–12cm long, which appear long after the leaves open.

Male flowers: minute with long stamens, growing in clusters towards the tip of the catkin.

Female flowers: in groups of 1–3 at the base of the catkin; each is surrounded by a green spiny cup from which slender white styles protrude.

Fruit: shiny red-brown nuts grouped in pairs or threes in a yellow-green

Sweet Chestnut

summer and autumn leaves

catkins

nut

immature fruit

winter

59

Beech
female flowers
male flowers

Left: A beech wood in spring, with a sweet chestnut in the foreground. Notice how little grows on the floor.

husk, 3 by 4cm, covered with radiating spines. The nuts are released when the husk splits.
Uses: the nuts are eaten roasted and used to make flour, bread, etc., and for fattening livestock. The timber — strong, durable, but easily split — is used for fencing, hop poles, posts, rough furniture, sleepers, etc.

BEECH *(Fagus sylvatica)*

Native to most of Europe (except northern Scandinavia), the beech is a dominant forest tree; it is also widely planted for ornament, shelter, hedges, and timber. It grows to 30m.
Crown: slender and conical, becoming rounded with spreading branches.
Bark: smooth and silvery-grey.
Buds: slender and pointed, 2cm long, covered with brown papery scales.
Leaves: oval with a pointed tip, wavy margins, and 5 to 7 parallel veins on each side; 10 by 7cm. Clear green and silky at first, they become dark shiny green above and paler beneath with hairs on the larger veins, turning pale yellow and finally rich orange-brown before falling.
Male and female flowers grow in separate clusters on the same tree and open with the leaves.

Male flowers: rounded greenish-yellow clusters, each of about 15 tiny flowers, on long drooping stalks.
Female flowers: in a rounded green head on a short stiff hairy stalk.
Fruit: a pointed green husk, 2·5cm long, covered with soft green hairs; turns brown and splits into 4 to release 1 to 2 shiny brown seeds (nuts), triangular in section.
Uses: the strong, hard, fine-grained wood, bright buff with brown flecks, is used for furniture and turnery (e.g. tool handles, bowls, spoons, chair legs); the nuts provide mast for pigs, cattle, and poultry.

Beech
winter bud
ripe fruit in husk
autumn

61

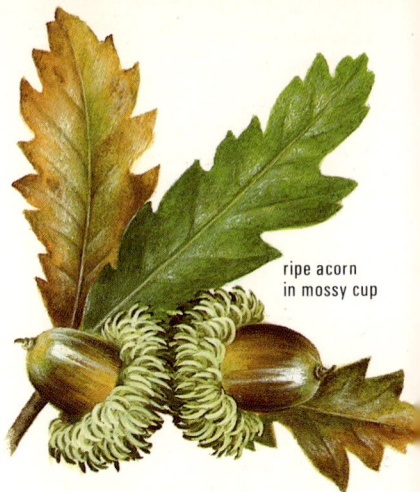

Turkey Oak

female flower

male catkins

ripe acorn in mossy cup

TURKEY OAK
(Quercus cerris)

The Turkey oak, native to south-west Asia and south and central Europe, is widely naturalized in Europe. The fastest growing of the oaks, it is widely planted for shade and ornament; it grows to 38m.

Crown: wide and broadly domed with straight up-growing branches.

Bark: dull dark-grey and roughly cracked.

Buds: pale brown and downy, surrounded by long twisted whiskers.

Leaves: variable, but usually with 7 to 14 deep triangular lobes down each side; 9–12 by 3–5cm. Borne on hairy stalks, 2cm long, the leaves are rough and dull green, becoming shiny, above; paler and woolly beneath.

Male flowers: in catkins, 5–6cm long, maturing from red to yellow.

Female flowers: oval, 5mm long, with dark-red stigmas surrounded by yellowish scales.

Fruit: narrow egg-shaped acorns, 2·5 by 1·4cm, either stalkless or on very short stalks and surrounded by a mossy cup, 1cm deep, with long pointed pale-green scales.

HOLM OAK *(Quercus ilex)*

This evergreen south European oak is widely planted for shelter and ornament, especially by the sea, being resistant to salty winds and pollution in towns; it grows to 30m.

Crown: dense and rounded, usually with a short trunk and straight up-growing branches.

Bark: brownish-black to black, cracked into small square plates.

Shoots: slender, dull greyish-brown, and woolly.

Buds: fawn and downy, 1–2mm long.

Leaves: vary from long and narrow to oval, with spiny-toothed, wavy, or smooth margins; 5–10 by 3–8cm. The upper surface is rough and shiny blackish-green, the lower surface greyish-green and densely hairy; the leafstalks are woolly and 1–2cm long.

Holm Oak

Male flowers: in pale-gold catkins, 4—7cm long.

Female flowers: grey-green and hairy with pink tips, 2mm long, growing on woolly stalks in clusters of 2 to 3.

Fruit: light-green acorns, 1·5—2cm long, with deep cups covered with rows of grey-haired fawn scales.

Uses: the hard heavy tough highly figured wood is used for wheels, joinery, vine-props, fuel, and charcoal; the bark is used for tanning leather and dyeing.

CORK OAK *(Quercus suber)*

Native to south Europe and North Africa, the evergreen cork oak is planted for ornament in parks and gardens as well as commercially (mainly in Portugal and south-west Spain) for its corky bark; grows to 20m.

Crown: domed and spreading, with low heavy twisting branches.

Bark: very rugged, with thick spongy ridges of pale brown or pale grey cork between wide dark cracks. Stripped trunks are pinkish-red.

Leaves: oval and pointed, with 5—6 shallow spine-tipped lobes on each side; 4—7 by 2—3cm. Blackish-green above and densely hairy beneath, they have hairy stalks, 1cm long.

Fruit: acorns, 1·5—3cm long, in deep cups with spreading upper scales.

Uses: cork, removed from the trunk every 8—10 years, is used for bungs, shoe soles, flooring, floats, life buoys, etc. The heavy wood is used for joinery and fuel.

Holm Oak

ripening acorns

Cork Oak

ripening acorn

underside of leaf

bark of cork oak

Sessile Oak

stalkless acorns

SESSILE or DURMAST OAK

(Quercus petraea)

The sessile oak — native to Europe (including Britain) and west Asia — forms forests over much of its natural range. It grows best on light acid soils and reaches a height of 30—40m.

Crown: open and domed, with straight branches radiating from a straight trunk.

Bark: grey, with fine, usually vertical, cracks and ridges.

Leaves: oblong, with a wedge-shaped base and 5 to 9 pairs of rounded lobes; 8—12 by 4—5cm. Dark green and leathery, they are borne on long yellow stalks (1—2cm).

Male flowers: in slender pale-green catkins.

Female flowers: tiny and greenish-white, with red-purple stigmas.

Fruit: rounded acorns, either stalkless or on very short stalks (5—10mm), ripening from green to brown.

Uses: (timber) see Pedunculate oak.

PENDUNCULATE or COMMON OAK

(Quercus robur)

The most widespread European oak: a long-lived slow-growing tree occurring in forests, woods, parks, and gardens all over Europe, from Spain to North Africa, north-east Russia, and south-west Asia; it grows to 45m. It can be distinguished from the sessile oak by the following features.

Crown: wide and domed, with wide-

Pendunculate Oak

Pendunculate Oak

stalked acorns

spreading branches (the lower ones are massive and twisted).

Leaves: oblong, with an ear-like lobe at the base on each side of the stalk and 4–5 pairs of rounded lobes with wavy or toothed margins; 10–12 by 7–8cm. Borne on short stalks (4–10mm), they are dull dark green above and paler beneath, turning rich orange-brown in autumn.

Fruit: acorns, 1·5–4cm long, with shallow cups, usually growing in pairs on stalks 4–8cm long. They mature from whitish-green to dark brown.

Uses: strong heavy timber, with white sapwood and golden-brown heart-wood, is durable and resistant; used for furniture, fencing, gates, railway carriages, panelling, chests, etc., and, in the past, for shipbuilding. The bark is used in tanning leather and the acorns provide mast for pigs.

RED OAK

(Quercus rubra; Quercus borealis)

This oak from eastern North America is commonly planted in Europe as an ornamental tree, for its attractive autumn foliage; for shelter; and, particularly in central Europe, for timber. It grows to 35m.

Crown: broad and domed, with straight radiating branches and a short straight trunk.

Bark: smooth and silvery-grey.

Leaves: oblong, 12–22cm long, with a pointed base and tip and 4 to 5 sharply angled lobes on each side, the tip of each lobe extending into a bristle. Borne on yellow stalks, 2–5cm long, the leaves turn from pale yellow to dark green above, pale grey beneath, and become dull red or red-brown in autumn.

Fruit: flat-based dark red-brown acorns, 2 by 2cm, in shallow scaly cups with incurved rims and stout 1-cm stalks.

summer and autumn leaves

autumn   **Red Oak**   ripe acorns

ELM FAMILY
(Ulmaceae)

Smooth-leaved Elm

SMOOTH-LEAVED ELM
(Ulmus carpinifolia)

Native to Europe, North Africa, and south-west Asia, this species is the common elm of continental Europe; it grows to 30m.

Crown: tall, narrow, and domed, with the branches growing up nearly vertically from the trunk and arching over into long hanging branchlets.

Bark: grey-brown, with long deep vertical cracks and long thick ridges; bark on the branches has fine black vertical cracks.

Shoots: pale brown, slender, and hairless.

Buds: egg-shaped, dark red, and hairy.

Leaves: oval, 6–8cm long, with a pointed tip, an oblique base, and toothed margins. Borne on hairy stalks 5mm long, the leaves are bright shiny green above and turn yellow in autumn.

Flowers and fruit: small red flowers with white stigmas appear before the leaves and develop into transparent winged fruits with the seed towards the tip of the membrane.

DUTCH ELM
(Ulmus hollandica var. *hollandica)*

One of many hybrids between the smooth-leaved elm and the wych elm, this tree is quite commonly planted in Europe; grows to 35m. Like nearly all other European elms it is susceptible to Dutch elm disease, which is caused by a fungus carried

Smooth-leaved Elm

ripe fruit

Above: Elm trees that have been killed by Dutch elm disease. The beetles that carry the disease spend their early lives tunnelling under the bark, and the bark of the affected trees gradually falls away, as seen here.

Below: The tunnels made under the bark by the elm bark beetle.

by the elm bark beetle and results in yellowing and shrivelling of the leaves and dying of the branches.

Crown: open, with wide-spreading twisting branches growing up from the trunk.

Bark: brown or grey-brown, cracked into small plates; the oldest trees have fluted trunks.

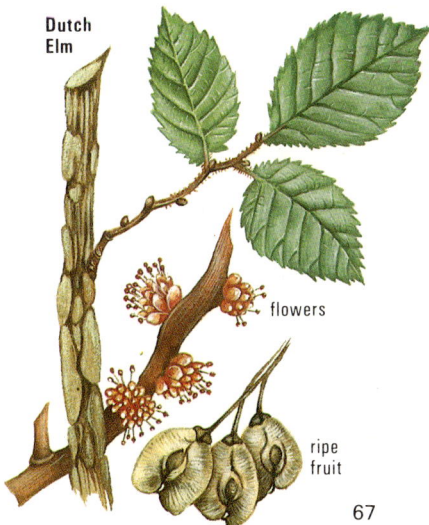

Dutch Elm

flowers

ripe fruit

67

Shoots: stout, brown, and initially covered with long hairs.

Buds: egg-shaped and shiny red-brown.

Leaves: oval, usually with a pointed tip, oblique base, and doubly toothed margins; 12–15 by 8cm. Borne on pinkish hairy stalks, 1cm long, the leaves are smooth and dark green above with stiff hairs on the veins beneath.

Flowers and fruit: dark red flowers develop into winged fruits, 2cm long, with the seed near the edge of the membrane. Appearing before the leaves, the fruits ripen from pale yellow-green to brown.

WYCH ELM

(Ulmus glabra)

Native to northern and central Europe and west Asia, the wych elm grows naturally in woods and hedgerows and is often planted in exposed situations and polluted atmospheres; it grows to 40m.

Crown: broadly domed, with branches

ripening fruit

Wych Elm

Wych Elm

flowers

winter twig

fruit

bark of wych elm

68

spreading and arching out from low down the trunk, which is often forked.
Bark: smooth and silvery-grey in young trees, becoming brown with a network of broad grey-brown ridges.
Shoots: stout and dark red-brown, covered with hairs when young.
Buds: pointed and dull red-brown with a covering of reddish hairs.
Leaves: oval, with a pointed tip, double-toothed margins, and an unequal base (the base on one side forms a rounded lobe that covers the stalk); 10–18 by 6–9cm. Borne on thick hairy stalks, 2–5mm long, the leaves are dark green and very rough above, paler with soft hairs beneath.

summer and autumn leaves

Flowers and fruit: dark purplish-red flowers grow in dense clusters that appear before the leaves. They develop into round winged fruits, 2–5cm wide with the seed at the centre of the membrane, which ripen from light green to brown.
Uses: the pliable strong wood is used for boat- and carriage-building, tool handles, shafts, and furniture.

ENGLISH ELM

(Ulmus procera)

This elm is native to Britain and occurs in many varieties and local forms in southern and central Europe; it grows to 35m.
Crown: tall, narrow, and domed, with massive twisting branches growing upwards from high up on the trunk.
Bark: dark brown or grey, deeply cracked into small square plates.
Shoots: long, slender, reddish-brown, and densely hairy.
Buds: pointed, dark brown, and downy; 2–3mm.
Leaves: rounded, or oval and pointed,

English Elm

bark of English elm

fruit

flowers

with double-toothed margins, an oblique base (one side may be lobed), and 10 to 12 pairs of veins; 4–10 by 3·5–7cm. Borne on 5mm downy stalks, they are dark green and rough with hairs on the upper surface and turn yellow or bright golden in autumn.
Flowers and fruit: dark purplish-red flowers with tufts of stamens appear before the leaves. They develop into sterile winged fruits, with the seed close to the notched tip of the rounded membrane, which mature from pale green to brown. The tree is propagated by root suckers.
Uses: the reddish-brown timber is strong, firm, heavy, and does not split easily; used for coffins, indoor and outdoor furniture, and – since it is durable under water – for bridges, piles, and groynes. The inner bark has medicinal properties.

MULBERRY FAMILY *(Moraceae)*

FIG
(Ficus carica)

Native to west Asia, the fig is widely cultivated – both as an important fruit crop (mainly in south Europe) and for shelter and ornament (it is often trained against walls); it grows to about 10m.
Crown: spreading, with stout knobbly upswept branches.
Bark: smooth and metallic grey, finely patterned in darker grey.
Leaves: thick and leathery, up to 30 by 25cm, with a heart-shaped base and 3 to 5 coarsely toothed lobes, the middle lobe being the largest. Borne on stalks 5–10cm long, they are dark green and rough with hairs above and hairy beneath.
Flowers: tiny, enclosed in a fleshy pear-shaped structure with a small hole at the top through which pollinating insects enter.
Fruit: dark green and pear-shaped, becoming larger and either violet or blackish when ripe.
Uses: the fruit is eaten either fresh or dried; it also has laxative properties.

ripe fruit

unripe fruit

Fig

BLACK or COMMON MULBERRY

(Morus nigra)

Silk moth caterpillars feed on mulberry leaves.

The black mulberry, native to central and west Asia, is widely cultivated in south Europe for its fruit and is grown elsewhere mainly for ornament; it reaches a height of 12m.

Crown: low and broadly domed, with rough stout twisting branches arising from a short trunk.

Bark: dark orange, with wide cracks and many bosses and burrs.

Shoots: stout and downy, turning from pale green to brown.

Buds: stout and pointed, shiny dark purplish-brown.

Leaves: heart-shaped, with toothed or lobed margins; 8–12 by 6–8cm. Growing on stout hairy stalks, 1·5–2·5cm long, they are rough, hairy, and deep green above, paler and finely hairy beneath.

Flowers: male and female flowers grow in separate pale-coloured catkins, the males being short and stout and the females rounded.

Fruit: rounded and raspberry-like, made up of a cluster of tiny berries each surrounding a central seed. Green at first, they become orange-scarlet and finally deep blackish-red and sweet enough to eat.

bark of black mulberry

Black Mulberry

ripe fruit

71

MAGNOLIA FAMILY
(Magnoliaceae)

TULIP TREE
(Liriodendron tulipifera)

Native to eastern North America, the tulip tree is planted in America and parts of central Europe for its pale, easily-worked timber; elsewhere it is grown for ornament in parks and gardens. In Europe it reaches a height of 35m.

Crown: tall and narrow — columnar or conical — with regular branches supported on a straight trunk.

Bark: grey, with a network of shallow even ridges, aging to pale orange-brown.

Shoots: smooth and red-brown, with prominent leaf scars.

Buds: shiny red-brown and laterally flattened; 1cm long.

Leaves: 4-lobed, 10–15 by 15–20cm, and very distinctive; the tip of the leaf between the two terminal lobes is cut straight across and has a shallow central notch. Borne on long (5–10cm) stalks, the leaves are rich glossy green above and paler beneath, turning bright gold or rich brown in autumn.

Tulip Tree

Flowers: tulip-like (4–5cm long, 6–8cm across), with 3 green sepals and 6 petals (each pale green with a broad orange band near its base), inside which is a central greenish cone (bearing the styles) surrounded by many fleshy yellow stamens.

Fruit: a brown papery erect cone-like structure, which splits to release the individual winged fruits, each bearing 1 to 2 seeds.

bud

Tulip Tree

ripening fruit

N.B.

EVERGREEN MAGNOLIA

(Magnolia grandiflora)

This evergreen species — native to the south-eastern USA — is widely cultivated for ornament, being planted in streets, parks, and gardens in southern Europe and against walls in cooler regions; it grows to a height of 10m.
Crown: broad and conical.
Bark: smooth and dark grey.
Shoots: fawn, densely covered with long rust-coloured hairs.
Buds: conical, greenish-brown with a brown tip; 1·5cm long.
Leaves: oval, often with wavy margins, tapering to a point at base and tip; 8–16 by 5–9cm. Borne on stout hairy stalks, 2–2·5cm long, they are thick and leathery, glossy green above with rust-coloured hairs beneath.
Flowers: fragrant and cup-shaped, 15–25cm across, with 6 thick white spreading 'petals' (sepals and petals are not differentiated); they are borne over a long period from summer to late autumn.
Fruit: conical, 5 by 3cm, made up of purplish-green hairy scales (the individual fruits) and borne on a stout curved orange-brown stalk.

MAGNOLIA x SOULANGEANA

Magnolia x soulangeana

One of the most popular of the cultivated magnolias, this small tree is a hybrid between two Chinese species:
the lily tree (*Magnolia liliiflora*) and *Magnolia denudata*; grows to a height of 10m. It is very adaptable, tolerating polluted atmospheres and poor soils.
Crown: low and spreading.
Shoots and buds: downy.
Leaves: oblong and pointed-tipped, often broadest at or below the middle; 10–15cm long.
Flowers: large and tulip-shaped; the petals (and usually also the sepals) are white, tinged with rose-purple at the base on the outside. There are many horticultural varieties, differing in the colour and size of their flowers.

Evergreen Magnolia

Magnolia x Soulangeana

buds

LAUREL FAMILY *(Lauraceae)*

Sweet Bay

male flowers

female flowers

fruit

SWEET BAY or BAY LAUREL

(Laurus nobilis)

In its native Mediterranean region this attractive evergreen tree reaches a height of 20m; it is widely grown elsewhere as an ornamental pot plant or shrub. Laurel leaves — worn in wreathes as a sign of victory or honour in classical times — are today used in cooking to season food.

Crown: dense and conical, with spreading up-growing branches.
Bark: smooth and blackish, with paler cracks in older trees.
Leaves: lance-shaped with wavy margins and dark-red basal veins; 5–10 by 2·5–3cm. Borne on dark-red stalks, 6mm long, they are leathery and very dark green above, yellow-green beneath, and aromatic when crushed.
Flowers and fruit: pale yellow inconspicuous flowers, 1cm across, develop into shiny berries, 8–10mm across, ripening from green to black.

PLANE FAMILY *(Platanaceae)*

LONDON PLANE

(Platanus x hispanica;
Plantanus x acerifolia)

A fast-growing hybrid between the Oriental plane and the American plane *(Platanus occidentalis)*, this tree is widely planted for shade and ornament in city streets and squares; it is resistant to pollution, thrives in restricted rooting space, and withstands heavy pruning. Grows to 35m.
Crown: domed, with large spreading branches supported on a long trunk.
Bark: smooth, thin, and grey-brown,

flaking off to reveal greenish or yellow patches.
Shoots: pale green, becoming stout and brown.
Buds: concial and red-brown, with a large protruding base and covered with a single scale.
Leaves: 5-lobed, each lobe being triangular with coarsely toothed margins. Borne on red-brown tube-like stalks, the leaves are bright shiny green above and paler beneath.
Flowers: male and female flowers grow in separate rounded clusters hanging on long stalks on the same

tree. The males are yellow; the females crimson.

Fruit: in brown globular clusters, 8cm across, that remain on the tree all winter and break up the following spring. Each fruit is 1cm long with a style projecting from the top and a parachute of yellow hairs at the bottom.

Uses: the pinkish-brown wood is used for veneers, being beautifully marked and taking polish well.

female flower clusters

male flower clusters

fruit

fruit cluster

London Plane

bark of London plane

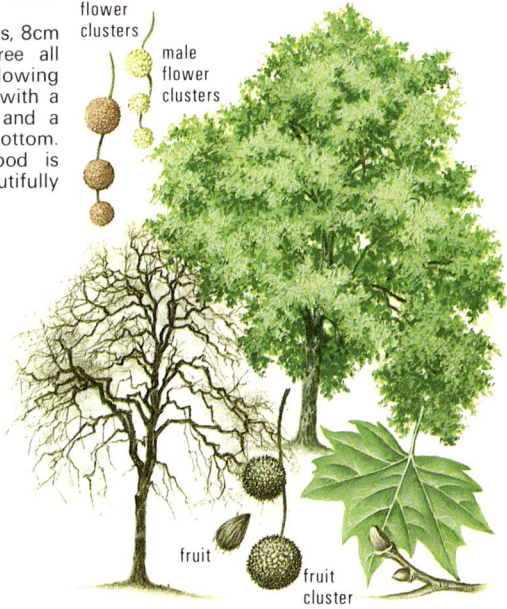

ORIENTAL PLANE

(Platanus orientalis)

Native to south-eastern and eastern Europe, Asia Minor, and India, the Oriental plane is often planted for shade and ornament in southern and eastern Europe; grows to 30m. Slower growing than the London plane and less tolerant of pollution, it can be distinguished from this tree by its leaves.

Leaves: 5- to 7-lobed, 18 by 8cm; the lobes are longer and narrower than those of the London plane. Borne on yellowish stalks, 5cm long, each with a thick red base, the leaves turn from pale orange-brown to yellow-green and finally to pale bronze-purple.

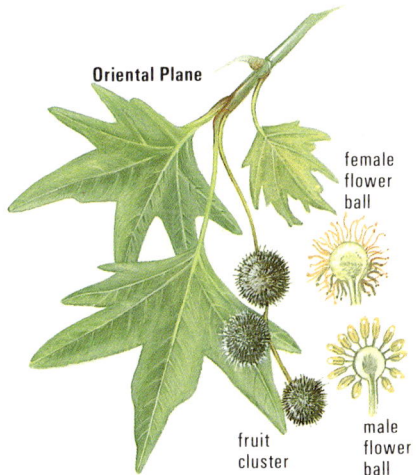

Oriental Plane

female flower ball

male flower ball

fruit cluster

ROSE FAMILY *(Rosaceae)*

Distributed all over the world, this vast family contains over 2000 species of trees, shrubs, and herbaceous plants, including all the important fruit trees. The members are distinguished by their flowers, which have 4–5 petals and an equal number of stamens, and their leaves with stipules at their bases.

HAWTHORN or MAY

(Crataegus monogyna)

This small spiny tree is very widely distributed in Europe, growing in thickets, hedgerows, and at the edges of woods; it is also planted as a windbreak and boundary hedge. It reaches a height of 10m.

Crown: spreading or rounded, with intertwining branches.

Bark: smooth and brown at first, becoming darker, rugged, and often fluted.

Shoots: dark purple-red or reddish-brown with straight thorns, 1–2·5cm long.

Buds: very small, reddish-black, and scaly.

Leaves: divided into 3 to 7 deep lobes with smooth or sparsely toothed margins; up to 8 by 7cm (usually 3·5 by

Hawthorn

ripe fruit

flower

Hawthorn

thorny twig

fruit

4cm). Borne on stalks 3·5cm long, the leaves are shiny green above and have tufts of down or hairs at the bases of the veins beneath.

Flowers: 8–15mm across, with 5 white overlapping petals, purple-tipped stamens, and one style; they grow in dense fragrant clusters of 16 or more.

Fruit: round, 8–10mm across, with a persistent style at the tip and containing (usually) one nutlet; ripens from green to dark red.

Uses: the heavy dense wood has been used for tool handles, mallet heads, and other small articles; makes good charcoal.

Red Hawthorn

MIDLAND or
RED HAWTHORN

*(Crataegus laevigata;
Crataegus oxyacantha)*

Similar to the previous species, this hawthorn can be distinguished by the following features:

Leaves: have shorter blunter lobes that are always toothed; there are no tufts on the lower surface.

Flowers: have 2 to 3 styles; cultivated ornamental varieties have red or pink, often double, flowers.

Fruit: has 2 to 3 persistent styles at the tip and encloses 2 to 3 nutlets.

MEDITERRANEAN
MEDLAR

(Crataegus azarolus)

Widely distributed in the Mediterranean region, this shrub or small tree is cultivated for its fruit in southern Europe; grows to a height of 4–12m.

Shoots: downy.

Leaves: pale green in colour, 3–7cm long, divided into blunt lobes usually without teeth and with hairs on the lower surface.

Flowers: small and white, with purple-tipped stamens, growing in downy clusters 5–7·5cm across.

Mediterranean Medlar

Fruit: large (2—2·5cm across) and round, orange-red or yellow, and containing 1 to 3 nutlets.

Uses: the fruit, which has a pleasant slightly acid taste, is made into jams and jellies.

CRAB APPLE

(Malus sylvestris)

The crab apple commonly grows in woods, thickets, and hedgerows of Europe and south-west Asia; it reaches a height of 10m. One of the species from which the orchard apple was derived, it is often grown as a rootstock on which garden varieties are grafted; some forms of crab apple are grown as flowering ornamentals.

Crown: dense, low, and domed, with many twisting spiny branches.

Bark: greyish-brown or dark brown, splitting into small thin square plates.

Shoots: ribbed and often thorny; dark purple above, pale brown beneath.

Buds: small (4—5mm) and pointed, dark purple and covered with grey hairs.

Leaves: oval, with a rounded or wedge-shaped base, pointed tip, and toothed margins; 5—6 by 3—4cm. Borne on downy grooved stalks, 2·5cm

Crab Apple

long, they are bright green above, paler and downy beneath.

Flowers: small, with 5 white petals, usually tinged with pink, and many yellow stamens; they grow in clusters from short spurs.

Fruit: globular, 2·5 by 2·8cm, with a hollow at each end and a central 'core' containing brown seeds (pips). The apples are glossy yellow-green

Crab Apple

with white spots and become speckled or flushed with red in autumn.

Uses: the fruit, though too sour to be eaten, is made into crab-apple jelly; the red-brown wood — hard, tough, and fine-grained — is used for ornamental carving, mallet handles.

MEDLAR
(Mespilus germanicus)

Native to south-eastern Europe and western and central Asia, the medlar has long been cultivated, especially in western and central Europe, for its fruit; it reaches a height of 6m.

Crown: low and spreading, with tangled branches.

Bark: grey-brown and deeply cracked into oblong plates that flake off.

Shoots: downy; they sometimes develop spines.

Leaves: oblong, with a pointed tip and smooth or toothed margins; 15 by 5cm. The upper surface is dull green, with indented veins, and is sometimes hairy; the lower surface is paler and densely hairy. The leaves are borne on very short (5mm) hairy stalks.

Flowers: stalkless, 3—6cm across, with 5 broad white petals, 5 long

Medlar

(4cm) green sepals, and many brown-tipped stamens.

Fruit: globular, 5—6cm across, ripening from green to brown. Persistent sepals surround an open pit at the tip through which the brown 'seeds' (actually individual fruits) can be seen.

Uses: the fruit is edible only when soft and over-ripe; it can also be made into a jelly. The wood is hard and fine-grained.

ripe fruit

Medlar

WILD CHERRY
or GEAN *(Prunus avium)*

In its wild state this tree grows in woodlands and thickets in Europe (except northern and Mediterranean regions), west Asia and North Africa; it reaches a height of 20m. It is the ancestor of all cultivated forms of sweet cherry and is widely grown in many varieties both for its fruit and for its blossom and attractive autumn foliage.

Crown: spreading, with branches growing up from a tall straight trunk.
Bark: purplish-grey, marked with horizontal orange-brown corky ridges and peeling off in thin horizontal strips.
Shoots: greyish-brown.
Buds: shiny red-brown and pointed.
Leaves: oval, with a pointed tip, finely-toothed margins, and 2 glands near the base; 10 by 4·5—7cm. Drooping from stalks 2—3·5cm long, which are red above and yellow beneath, the leaves are pale green (downy beneath) and turn crimson or yellow in autumn.
Flowers: white and sweetly scented, growing on slender stalks in clusters at the tips of the branches.
Fruit: rounded and shiny, 2·5cm across, growing on a red-brown stalk 3·5cm long and ripening from green to bright red and finally purple. Sweet-tasting when ripe, they are dispersed by birds.
Uses: the fruit of cultivated varieties is eaten fresh, made into jams, liqueurs, etc.; the golden-brown wood is heavy, hard, and tough and prized for furniture and turned articles (such as bowls, pipes and similar musical instruments).

'KANZAN'
FLOWERING CHERRY
(Prunus 'Kanzan')

This flowering cherry is a widely grown ornamental tree; it is one of a group of Japanese cultivated varieties thought to be related to, and possibly derived from, the Japanese cherry *(Prunus serrulata)*; it grows to 6m.
Crown: spreading, with up-growing branches that are widely arching in old trees.
Leaves: oval, with a pointed tip and margins with whiskery teeth; 18 by 9cm. Borne on red stalks, 3cm long, they open bright red, turning dark

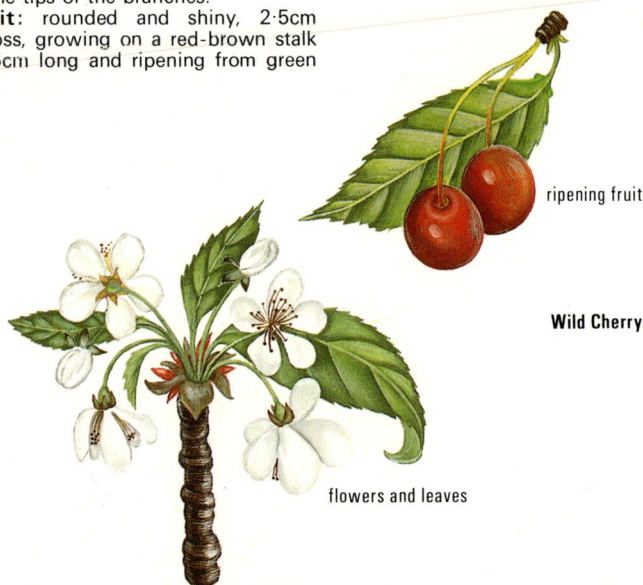

ripening fruit

Wild Cherry

flowers and leaves

80

green above, whitish beneath, and finally gold or pinkish in autumn.
Flowers: pink and semi-double, growing in billowing clusters.

BIRD CHERRY

(Prunus padus)

Native to northern and central Europe and Asia Minor, the bird cherry grows in woods, especially by streams, as a low shrub or a tree up to 15m tall.
Crown: rounded, with sharply ascending upper branches and spreading or drooping lower ones.
Bark: smooth and dark brown, with a strong unpleasant smell of bitter almonds.
Shoots: olive green, turning dark brown.
Buds: slender and sharply pointed; shiny brown.
Leaves: oval, with a pointed base and tip and finely-toothed margins; 10 by 7cm. Borne on dark red stalks, 2cm long, they are dull green above and pale green beneath, turning pale yellow or red in autumn.
Flowers: small, white, and fragrant, grouped in long (8–15cm) spreading or drooping clusters.
Fruit: globular and shiny, 8mm across, ripening from green to black. Bitter-tasting, they are dispersed by birds.

The 'double' flowers of the ornamental cherry tree known as 'Kanzan'.

bark of bird cherry

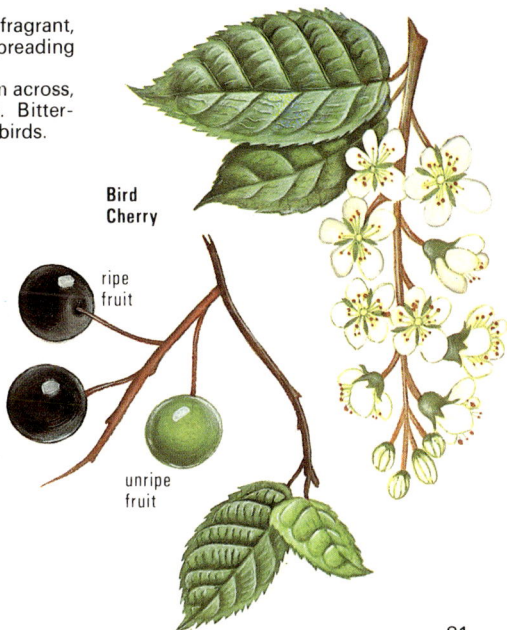

Bird
Cherry

ripe
fruit

unripe
fruit

81

ALMOND

(Prunus dulcis;
Prunus amygdalus)

unripe
fruit

Almond

A native of west Asia and North Africa, this small tree is widely cultivated – in warm regions for its nuts and elsewhere for ornament in gardens, parks, etc.; it reaches a height of about 6m.

Crown: open and rounded, with up-growing branches.

Bark: purplish-black, deeply cracked into small square plates.

Leaves: oval, 7–12cm long, with a pointed tip and finely toothed margins. Dark green or yellowish-green in colour, they are often folded along the midrib into a V shape.

Flowers: pink, 3–5cm across, with 5 petals and many stamens; they open well before the leaves. Some cultivated varieties have white or double flowers.

Fruit: oval and pale green, 4cm long, splitting when ripe to reveal a pale brown stone within which is the edible kernel.

Uses: nuts from the sweet almond are eaten raw and used for cooking, flavouring, etc.; bitter almonds yield almond oil, used for flavouring. The hard reddish wood of the tree is used for veneers.

Blackthorn

BLACKTHORN or SLOE *(Prunus spinosa)*

The blackthorn is widely distributed in Europe and parts of Asia, growing in hedgerows, on waste ground, scrub, hillsides, etc.; it produces suckers and grows to a height of 4m.

Crown: dense and upright, with a tangled mass of thorny branches.

Bark: black; in old trees it is deeply cracked into small square plates.

Shoots: downy.

Buds: small, oval, and pointed; reddish-purple to black in colour.

Leaves: small (4cm long), dull green, and oval, with a bluntly pointed tip and shallow-toothed margins.

Flowers: white, 1–1·5cm across, with 5 petals and long orange-tipped stamens; they usually open well before the leaves.

Fruit: globular, 1·5–2cm across, ripening from green to purple-black with a waxy bloom; the green flesh has a very bitter taste.

Uses: the fruit is used for jams and jellies, flavouring gin, and is fermented into sloe wine; the tough wood, with pale yellow sapwood and dark brown heartwood, is made into walking sticks and handles.

Myrobalan

ripe fruit

MYROBALAN or CHERRY PLUM

(Prunus cerasifera)

Native to the Balkans and central Asia, the myrobalan is planted in central Europe for its edible fruit (the cultivated plum is probably a hybrid between this tree and the blackthorn); it grows to about 8m. There are also several early-flowering cultivated varieties, which are widely grown as ornamentals.

Crown: open and spreading.

Bark: brownish-black.

Shoots: smooth and glossy green.

Leaves: oval with blunt-toothed margins; 4–7cm long. Borne on purple-green stalks, 1cm long, the leaves are glossy green above, paler and matte beneath (some ornamental varieties have reddish leaves).

Flowers: white, 2cm across, with 5 petals; cultivated ornamental varieties have white or pink flowers.

Fruit: globular and grooved down one side, ripening from pale glossy green to yellow or red, and containing a flattish stone.

The densely-packed white flowers of the blackthorn or sloe open early in the spring, long before the leaves.

Whitebeam
in flower

WHITEBEAM

(Sorbus aria)

The whitebeam, native to southern and central Europe and parts of Britain, is found in woodlands, rocky regions, and on southern mountains; reaches a height of 25m. It grows well on chalk and limestone, and, because it withstands pollution, it is often planted in city streets.

Crown: domed, with up-swept radiating branches.

Bark: smooth and grey, developing shallow cracks and ridges with age.

Shoots: brown and hairy at first, becoming smooth and grey.

Buds: green, with brown-tipped scales and a white hairy tip; 2cm long.

Leaves: oval, with shallow-toothed or lobed margins; 8 by 5cm. The upper surface is dull green, the lower surface is densely covered with white hairs, giving the whole tree a glistening white appearance when the leaves first appear. The leaves turn yellow or pale brown in autumn and finally pale grey before falling.

Flowers: white, 1·5cm across, growing on white woolly stalks in clusters 5–8cm across.

Fruit: rounded, 8–15cm across, ripening from green to orange-red and finally deep scarlet; they are dispersed by birds.

Uses: the hard heavy tough wood — yellowish-white and fine-grained — is sometimes used for handles, spoons, etc.; the fruit is made into a jelly.

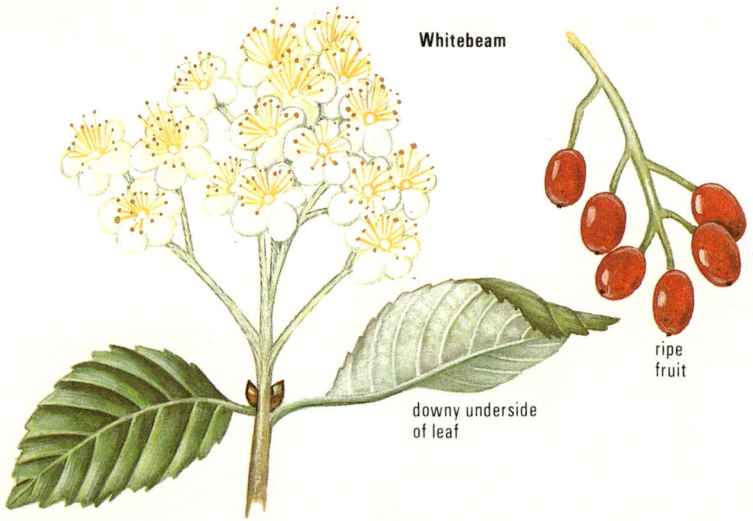

Whitebeam

downy underside of leaf

ripe fruit

ROWAN or MOUNTAIN ASH

(Sorbus aucuparia)

This attractive tree grows wild in woodlands and rocky mountainous regions of Europe, south-west Asia, and North Africa; it is also widely planted as an ornamental tree in streets, parks, and gardens. It reaches a height of 20m.

Crown: oval and open, with up-growing branches.

Bark: smooth and shiny silver-grey, becoming light grey-brown and marked with a network of thin scaly ridges.

Shoots: purplish- or brownish-grey, hairy at first, becoming smooth.

Buds: dark purple-brown, 1.7cm long, covered with grey hairs.

Leaves: compound, 22cm long, consisting of 5 to 7 pairs of leaflets and one terminal leaflet (each is oval, with toothed margins; 6 by 2cm). Hairy at first, they become smooth and deep green above, grey-green beneath; the leaves of some cultivated varieties turn bright red in autumn.

Flowers: creamy white and 5-petalled, 1cm across, growing on woolly stems in flat-topped sweetly scented clusters, 10–15cm across.

Fruit: round berries, 1cm across, maturing from yellow to orange and finally scarlet; they are dispersed by birds.

Uses: the fruit, rich in vitamin C, is made into jelly; the smooth hard purple-brown wood is used for carved and turned articles.

winter

Rowan

ripe fruit

summer and autumn leaves

Wild Service Tree   winter

ripe fruit

WILD SERVICE TREE
(Sorbus torminalis)

This tree is widely distributed in Europe (except the north), North Africa, and parts of Asia; it grows to a height of 25m.

Crown: conical when young, becoming domed and spreading, with upgrowing branches.

Bark: pale grey to black-brown; it cracks into thin plates that flake off.

Shoots: brown and shiny.

Buds: glossy green and globular; 4–5mm long.

Leaves: divided into 3 to 5 pairs of triangular toothed lobes that decrease in size towards the tip of the leaf; 10 by 8cm. Borne on yellowish-green stalks, 2–5cm long, the leaves are shiny deep green above and yellow-green beneath, turning yellow, deep red, and purple in autumn.

Flowers: 1·2cm across, with 5 white petals and yellow stamens; they are grouped into loose domed clusters, 10–12cm across.

Fruit: oval, 1cm or more long, ripening from green to brown with rust-coloured specks. Acid-tasting, they are said to have medicinal properties and have been used in the past as a cure for colic.

BASTARD SERVICE TREE   *(Sorbus x thuringiaca)*

A hybrid between the rowan (mountain ash) and the whitebeam, the bastard service tree is grown for ornament, mostly in town streets; it reaches a height of 15m.

Bastard Service Tree

ripe fruit

86

Crown: oval and upright, becoming dense and leaning to one side.
Bark: dull grey with shallow cracks.
Shoots: pink-grey with a purple tip.
Buds: dark red-brown; 8mm long.
Leaves: oblong, 11 by 7cm, with lobes that decrease in size towards the tip of the leaf; 1—4 pairs of toothed leaflets grow at the base of each leaf. Borne on stout red stalks, 2cm long, the leaves are dark grey-green above and white with down beneath.
Flowers: white, 1cm across, grouped in downy clusters, 6—10cm across.
Fruit: bright red, 1·2cm across, growing in clusters of 10 to 15.

TRUE SERVICE TREE

(Sorbus domestica)

The service tree — native to southern Europe, North Africa, and west Asia — is widely planted for ornament and (particularly in central Europe) for its fruit; it grows to a height of 20m. When not bearing fruit, it can be distinguished from the rowan — a similar species — by its bark and buds.
Crown: domed, with spreading level branches.
Bark: orange- to dark-brown, cracked (often deeply) into rectangular plates.
Buds: egg-shaped, glossy bright green, and resinous; 1cm long.
Leaves: compound, 15—22cm long, with 6 to 10 pairs of leaflets and one terminal leaflet, each oblong and

summer

Bastard Service Tree

sharply toothed, 3—6cm long, dark yellow-green above, downy beneath.
Flowers: 1·5—2cm across, with 5 cream-coloured petals, triangular sepals, and 5 styles; they grow in domed erect clusters, 10 by 14cm.
Fruit: globular or pear-shaped, 2—3cm long, ripening from green to brown. They are edible when over-ripe and are used in continental Europe for making alcoholic beverages.

True Service Tree

ripening fruit

PEAR *(Pyrus communis)*

The parent species from which the numerous orchard and garden varieties of pear are derived, this tree grows wild in woods, hedgerows, etc., of Europe and west Asia; it reaches a height of 20m.
Crown: slender, with a rounded top and up-growing branches.
Bark: grey-brown or black, breaking into small deep squares.
Shoots: brown, often downy, and sometimes thorny.
Leaves: oval to heart-shaped, 5–8cm long, with a pointed tip and smooth or toothed margins. Borne on long (2–5cm) stalks, they are glossy dark- or yellow-green.
Flowers: 2–4cm across, with 5 white petals and dark-red stamens; they grow in dense clusters, 5–8cm across, that open before the leaves.
Fruit: varies from globular to oblong, 2–4cm long, ripening from green to brown; the gritty flesh is sweet when ripe.
Uses: the hard compact pinkish-brown wood is used for furniture, turned articles, wood blocks, etc.; it also makes good fuel and charcoal.

WILLOW-LEAVED PEAR *(Pyrus salicifolia)*

Native to south-east Europe and west Asia, this pear is often planted as an ornamental in parks and gardens (usually as the variety *pendula*); grows to 8m.
Crown: domed, with slender hanging branches.

Willow-Leaved Pear

Pear

Leaves: long and narrow, 3–9 by 1–2cm, tapering to a point at base and tip. Growing on short (3–15mm) stalks, they are covered with silvery hairs at first, later becoming glossy green on the upper surface.
Flowers: white, 2cm across, growing in dense clusters on white woolly stalks.
Fruit: small and brown; 2–3cm long.

Right: The long, hanging flower clusters of the laburnum give the tree its other name of 'golden rain'. Like the other parts of the tree the flowers are poisonous.

PEA FAMILY *(Leguminosae)*

The 7000 or more species of this family – which includes peas, beans, and other herbaceous plants as well as trees and shrubs – are found all over the world. They are distinguished by their fruit – a pod. Because their roots bear nodules containing nitrogen-fixing bacteria, leguminous plants improve the fertility of the soil in which they grow.

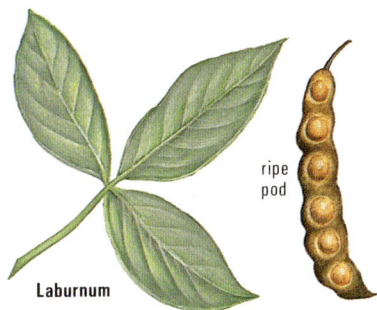

ripe pod

Laburnum

LABURNUM
(Laburnum anagyroides)

The common laburnum grows wild in woods and thickets in mountainous regions of southern and central Europe; it reaches a height of 7m. It is very widely planted as an ornamental tree in parks, gardens, and streets and has become naturalized in many regions. All parts of the tree, especially the seeds, are poisonous.

Crown: narrow, open, and irregular, with up-growing branches.

Bark: smooth; green at first, becoming

Laburnum

unripe pods

89

Locust Tree

winter

bark of locust tree

ripe pods

FALSE ACACIA or LOCUST TREE

(Robinia pseudoacacia)

greenish-brown.

Shoots: grey-green and covered with long grey hairs.

Buds: egg-shaped, pale grey-brown, and hairy.

Leaves: compound, with 3 oval pointed leaflets, 3—8cm long. Borne on stalks 2—6cm long, the leaves are greyish-green above, blue-grey and covered with silky hairs beneath.

Flowers: bright yellow and shaped like those of the pea, 2cm long, growing in hanging clusters, 10—30cm long.

Fruit: slender pods, 4—8cm long, containing black seeds. Hanging in bunches, they are hairy when young, becoming dark brown and hairless.

Native to eastern North America, the false acacia has long been planted in Europe as an ornamental tree in parks, gardens, etc. It grows well on sandy soils and is often planted to stabilize the soil; it reaches a height of 30m.

Crown: irregular and open, with twisted branches and a fluted and burred trunk.

Bark: smooth and brown in young trees, becoming dull grey and rugged, with a network of deep ridges and cracks, with age.

Shoots: dark red and ribbed, each with a pair of short spines at its base.

Buds: small and hidden by the leaf-stalks until autumn.

Leaves: compound, 15—20cm long,

made up of 3 to 7 pairs of oval leaf-lets and one terminal leaflet (each 2·5—4·5cm long). The leaves vary from yellow-green to light green and spines are often present at the base of the leafstalks.

Flowers: white and resembling those of the pea, growing in dense hanging fragrant clusters, 10—20cm long.

Fruit: dark brown pods, 5—10cm long, each containing 4 to 16 seeds; they hang from the branches in bunches well into winter.

Judas Tree

winter

JUDAS TREE

(Cercis siliquastrum)

Said to be the tree on which Judas Iscariot hanged himself, the beautiful Judas tree grows wild in rocky regions of southern Europe and western Asia. It is often planted — especially in warmer regions — for ornament in parks and gardens; it reaches a height of 10—12m.

Crown: low and irregularly domed.

Bark: purplish, becoming pinkish-grey with fine brown cracks.

Shoots: dark red-brown.

Buds: dark red, narrow, and conical, 3—5mm long.

Leaves: nearly circular, with a heart-shaped base and smooth margins; 8-12 by 10—12cm. Borne on stalks 5cm long, they are yellow- or dark-green above and paler beneath.

Flowers: rosy pink and resembling those of the pea, 2cm long, growing in clusters (often directly from the trunk) that open before the leaves have appeared.

Fruit: flat red-purple pods, becoming brown and remaining on the tree throughout winter.

Judas Tree

ripe pods

N.B.

SILVER WATTLE or MIMOSA *(Acacia dealbata)*

This beautiful fast-growing tree from south-east Australia is widely planted for ornament in southern and western Europe; it is also used by florists. In Europe it usually reaches a height of 8–12m (grows to 30m in Australia).
Crown: broad and conical.
Bark: blue-green in young trees, becoming pale brown and smooth and finally grey and fluted.
Shoots: slightly ribbed, greenish-white, and densely covered with down.
Leaves: fern-like, up to 12 by 4cm, made up of 10 to 12 pairs of leaflets, 3cm long, that point forwards and are themselves divided into about 30 pairs of soft needle-like leaflets, 3–4mm long. Blue- or yellow-green and covered with fine down, they give the tree a silvery appearance.
Flowers: small and bright yellow, grouped into globular heads, 3–5mm across, which grow in long branched clusters of 20 to 30.

HONEY LOCUST *(Gleditsia triacanthos)*

The honey locust — a spiny tree of North America — is quite widely planted for ornament in parks, gardens, etc., especially in southern and central Europe; grows to a height of 20m.
Crown: wide and spreading, with twisted smaller branches.
Bark: dark purple-grey, with wide shallow ridges and clusters of branched spines up to 30cm long. (Cultivated trees often lack spines.)
Leaves: either compound, 10–15cm long, with 7 to 18 pairs of oblong to lance-shaped leaflets (2–4cm long) with slightly toothed margins; or doubly compound, 20cm long, divided into 4 to 7 pairs of leaflets that are themselves made up of 11 pairs of smaller leaflets. The leaves are bright yellow-green or dark green and turn bright gold in autumn. The variety 'Sunburst' has golden leaves that turn yellowish-green in autumn.
Flowers: pale yellow-green and fra-

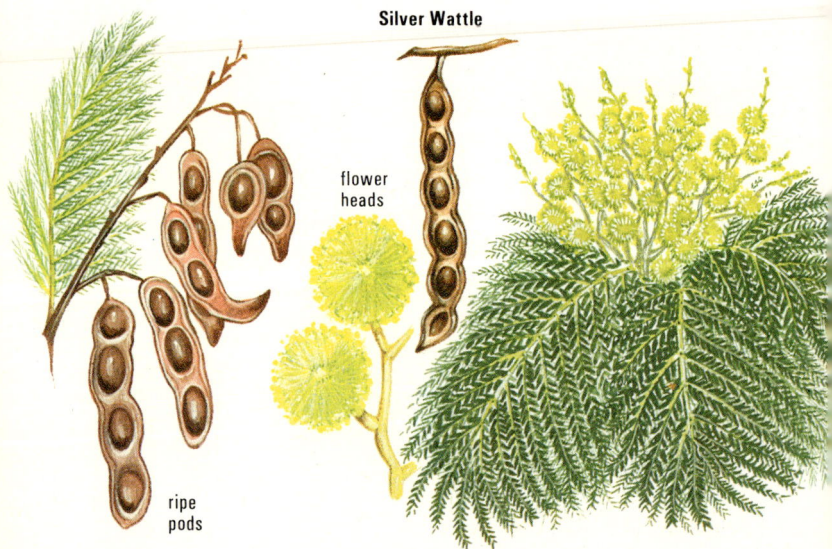

Silver Wattle

flower heads

ripe pods

Honey Locust

male flowers

unripe pods

The Sydney golden wattle in full flower, with dense bunches of sweet-scented flowers covering the branches.

grant, about 5–6mm long; male flowers grow in long (12cm) downy clusters, female flowers in separate, less crowded, clusters.

Fruit: long sickle-shaped twisted pods, 25–30 by 2–3cm, ripening from pale yellow-green to brown.

SYDNEY GOLDEN WATTLE *(Acacia longifolia)*

Another native of Australia, this small shrubby wattle is often planted for ornament and, in south-west Europe, for stabilizing sand dunes; reaches a height of 5m.

Shoots: stiff, angular, and hairless.

Leaves: narrow, blunt, and light green, 5–15cm long, each with 2 to 4 veins.

Flowers: small, bright yellow, and strongly scented, growing in cylindrical clusters, 2–6cm long, from the axils of the leaves.

ripe pod

Sydney Golden Wattle

CITRUS FAMILY
(Rutaceae)

This family includes over 1000 species, mostly of tropical and subtropical regions. The citrus trees – none of which are native to Europe – were originally from South East Asia but have been widely cultivated in warm regions (particularly the Mediterranean) since ancient times. They all have glossy evergreen leaves, whose glands secrete aromatic oils, and 5-petalled flowers.

LEMON *(Citrus limon)*

Lemon

Probably native to India, this small spiny tree is the least hardy of the citrus trees; grows to a height of 6–7m.
Crown: irregular and spreading.
Shoots: reddish and bearing stout spines.
Leaves: dark green and oval, with a pointed tip and crinkly or toothed margins. The leafstalks are jointed and narrowly winged.
Flowers: fragrant, growing singly or in pairs, and developing from reddish buds. The petals are white, tinged with purple on the outside, and there are 20 to 40 stamens. In some flowers both stamens and ovaries are functional; in others only the stamens are fertile.
Fruit: egg-shaped, with a nipple-like projection at the tip; the rind is pale yellow and the flesh acid-tasting. Lemons are used principally for beverages and flavouring.

GRAPEFRUIT
(Citrus paradisi)

The grapefruit is thought to be native to south-east China; it reaches a height of 10–15m.
Crown: rounded or pyramid-shaped.
Leaves: oval, with a pointed tip, smooth margins, and very broadly winged leafstalks (up to 1·5cm wide). The leaves, which often have spines in their axils, are light green when they

The heavy, ripe fruit of the grapefruit, ready for picking.

first open, becoming darker on the upper surface.

Flowers: white, growing either singly or in clusters.

Fruit: globular, 10–15cm across, with thick smooth pale-yellow or yellow-orange rind and sweet or slightly acid-tasting flesh.

CITRON *(Citrus medica)*

This small tree was the first citrus species to be brought from the Far East for cultivation in Europe.

Crown: irregular and spreading.

Leaves: oval, with toothed margins and rounded or narrowly winged leaf-stalks. Short spines grow in the axils of the leaves.

Flowers: large and fragrant, developing from purple buds, with pinkish-white outer petals and many stamens.

Fruit: oblong or oval and very large (15–25cm long), with very thick rough yellow rind and pale green or yellow flesh with a sweetish or acid taste. The rind is candied or preserved and used in confectionery, for flavouring cakes, etc.

The citron is slightly more pointed than the grapefruit, left.

Ripe Seville oranges, ready to be picked and made into marmalade.

SEVILLE ORANGE

(Citrus aurantium)

Similar to the sweet orange, this small tree can be distinguished chiefly by its fruit.

Crown: rounded or spreading.

Leaves: like those of the sweet orange, but the leafstalks are more broadly winged.

Flowers: white and fragrant, growing singly or in small clusters in the axils of the leaves.

Fruit: rounded, about 7·5cm across, but flattened slightly at both ends; the aromatic rind is orange or reddish-orange and rough, and the flesh is bitter-tasting.

Uses: the fruit is used for marmalade, beverages (including the liqueur curaçao), and confectionery (as candied peel); oil of Neroli, used in perfumery, is distilled from the flowers.

Seville Orange

Sweet Orange

TANGERINE
(Citrus nobilis; Citrus deliciosa)

The tangerine is a small spiny tree with distinctive fruits.
Leaves: narrow and oval, with a pointed tip and narrowly winged leafstalks.
Flowers: white, growing singly or in small clusters.
Fruit: rounded, 5–7·5cm across, and flattened or depressed at both ends. The rind — thin and bright orange — separates readily from the sweet-tasting flesh when the fruit is ripe.

SWEET ORANGE
(Citrus sinensis)

Native to China, the sweet orange is the most adaptable of all the citrus trees to growing at lower temperatures, although it is prone to attack by pests and disease; it reaches a height of 9–13m. As well as being grown for its fruit, it is a popular ornamental pot plant.
Crown: rounded or pyramid-shaped.
Leaves: oval, 7·5–10cm long, with a pointed tip, smooth margins, and narrowly winged leafstalks. The leaves are dark green above, paler beneath.
Flowers: white and fragrant, growing singly or in small clusters.
Fruit: rounded, with smooth yellow, orange, or orange-red rind and sweet-tasting flesh. It is eaten fresh, made into orange juice, or used for flavouring.

Tangerines are dark green before they ripen and acquire their orange colour.

QUASSIA FAMILY *(Simaroubaceae)*

TREE OF HEAVEN
(Ailanthus altissima)

This fast-growing Chinese tree is widely grown for shade and ornament in streets, parks, and gardens (it is naturalized in parts of southern and central Europe); it withstands pollution and is often planted for soil conservation. It reaches a height of 25m.
Crown: a tall loose irregular dome, with stout wavy up-growing branches supported on a straight trunk.
Bark: smooth, grey-brown to black, with white vertical streaks; it becomes dark grey and roughened with age.
Shoots: stout and orange-brown.
Buds: small and egg-shaped, maturing from red-brown to scarlet.
Leaves: compound, 30–60cm long, consisting of 5 to 22 pairs of leaflets. Each leaflet is narrow, oval, and pointed, 7–15cm long, with 1 to 3 large teeth on each side at the base with a large gland underneath each tooth. Borne on red stalks, 7–15cm

winter

Tree of Heaven

long, the leaves are deep red when they first open, becoming deep green above and paler beneath.
Flowers: small and greenish, growing in large clusters; male and female flowers often grow on separate trees.
Fruit: twisted wings, each with a seed in the centre; 4cm long. They grow in large hanging clusters, 30 by 30cm, ripening from yellow-green to bright orange-red.

ripe fruit

Tree of Heaven

97

BOX FAMILY *(Buxaceae)*

BOX *(Buxus sempervirens)*

The evergreen box, a native of southern and central Europe, parts of Britain, and North Africa, grows as a shrub or small tree on hillsides; it reaches a height of 10m. It is widely planted in parks, gardens, and churchyards, particularly as a screening and decorative hedge; it clips well and is commonly used for topiary work.

Crown: (tree form) dense and rather narrow, on a slender trunk.

Bark: thin and pale brown, patterned with small squares, becoming pale grey in old trees.

Shoots: green, covered with orange down; they are square in section.

Buds: domed, pale orange-brown, and hairy.

Leaves: hard, leathery, and oval, with a tendency to be inrolled; 1·5—3cm long. Borne on very short (1mm) stalks, they are glossy and dark green above, paler beneath.

Flowers: male and female flowers grow in separate clusters at the base of the leaves. They lack petals, consisting only of stamens (4 per flower) or styles (3 per flower).

Fruit: rounded 3-part capsules bearing the remains of the styles; they split when ripe to release small glossy black seeds.

Uses: the hard heavy close-grained wood is used for carving (e.g. chess pieces), engraving, tool handles, drawing instruments, etc.

fruit

Box

Box grows very slowly and so is useful for hedges and for topiary.

HOLLY FAMILY *(Aquifoliaceae)*

HOLLY *(Ilex aquifolium)*

This evergreen grows as a shrub or small tree in woods, thickets, and hedgerows in western, central, and southern Europe; it reaches a height of 10m. Since it withstands clipping, the holly is grown as a hedge in gardens; there are also many ornamental varieties with attractive foliage and berries.

Crown: conical and spired, with up-turned branches, in young trees; becomes dense and irregular with age.

Bark: smooth and silvery-grey, becoming rough and gnarled with age.

Shoots: bright green or purple; stout and grooved.

Buds: green, very small, and sharply pointed.

Leaves: very variable, but usually leathery and oval, 6–8cm long, with a pointed tip; glossy dark green above, bright green and matt beneath. Leaves on the lower branches have spiny margins, those higher up have wavy or smooth margins. Some cultivated ornamental varieties have variegated foliage.

Flowers: male and female flowers grow on separate trees in crowded fragrant clusters at the base of the leaves. Each flower is small (6–8mm across) and white, opening from a purple bud.

Fruit: poisonous berries, 7–10mm across, ripening from green to scarlet. Borne on a stalk 4–8mm long, each contains 3 to 4 black seeds. Some ornamental varieties have yellow berries.

Uses: the ivory-white wood — hard, heavy, and fine-grained — is valued for turned articles, inlay work, and carving.

Holly

Holly

N.B.

SPINDLE TREE FAMILY *(Celastraceae)*

Spindle Tree

SPINDLE TREE

(Euonymus europaeus)

The attractive spindle tree is found throughout Europe (except in the extreme north), growing as a shrub or small tree in woods, thickets, and hedgerows, especially on chalk or limestone soils; reaches a height of 6m.

Crown: much-branched, broad, and flat-topped.
Bark: smooth and green, becoming grey or pale brown with age.
Shoots: green and 4-angled, becoming rounded.
Buds: green and egg-shaped.
Leaves: oval to lance-shaped, 3–10cm long, with a pointed tip and finely toothed margins. Borne on stalks 6–12mm long, they are shiny blue-green above and paler beneath, turning yellow, russet, and crimson in autumn.
Flowers: small (1cm across), with 4 greenish-white petals and 4 stamens; they grow in loose long-stalked clusters of 3 to 8 at the base of the leaves.
Fruit: 4-lobed seed-pods, 10–15mm across, ripening from green to bright pink. When ripe they split to reveal the seeds, each covered by a fleshy orange-red coat (aril); the seeds themselves, which are poisonous, are white and surrounded by a pink seed coat.
Uses: the whitish wood is hard, smooth, and tough; it has been used for spindles, knitting needles, pegs, toothpicks, etc., and makes excellent artists' charcoal.

autumn leaves

Spindle Tree

ripe fruit

autumn

MAPLE FAMILY *(Aceraceae)*

Most of the trees in this family (which contains about 150 species) are maples (genus *Acer*). Their flowers – small and greenish-yellow – grow in clusters and their fruits consist of 2 wings joined by the seeds at their bases.

FIELD MAPLE

(Acer campestre)

Often growing as a small tree or shrub in hedgerows, especially on chalk or limestone soils, the hardy field maple is found throughout Europe, extending to southern Sweden, North Africa, and northern Persia; reaches a height of 25m. It is grown for ornament and hedges.

Crown: domed and usually low.
Bark: pale brown with wide cracks or split into squares; becomes darker with age.
Shoots: brown, covered with fine hairs and, later, corky ridges.
Buds: brown and hairy; 3mm long.
Leaves: up to 8 by 12cm, with 5 rounded lobes each with a shallow notch near the tip (the middle, largest, lobe has parallel sides or is wedge-shaped). Borne on slender green or pink stalks, 5–9cm long, the leaves open pinkish, becoming dark green above (paler beneath) and bright gold or reddish in autumn.
Flowers: grow in erect widely spaced clusters of about 10 and open with the leaves.
Fruit: horizontal wings, 5–6cm across, yellow-green tinged with crimson, ripening to brown.
Uses: the hard strong pale-brown wood is valued for carving and turned articles (bowls, etc.).

BOX ELDER or ASH-LEAVED MAPLE

(Acer negundo)

This North American maple is widely cultivated in Europe for shelter and ornament, being planted in town streets, parks, and gardens; short-lived and fast-growing, it reaches a height of 20m.

Crown: irregularly domed, leaning to one side with age.
Bark: smooth and grey-brown at first, becoming darker and cracked.
Shoots: green and straight, becoming covered with purple bloom in the second year.
Buds: small, white, and silky.

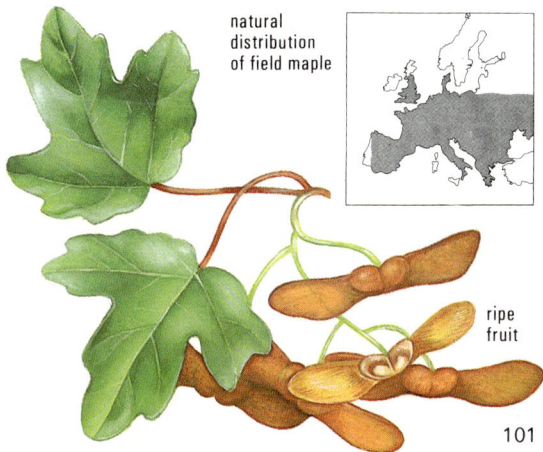

natural
distribution
of field maple

Field Maple

ripe fruit

Leaves: compound, up to 20 by 15cm, with 3 to 7 irregularly toothed leaflets. Borne on pale-yellow or pink stalks, 6—8cm long, the leaves are pale green, but the colour varies in ornamental varieties (var. *variegatum* has white-margined leaves).

Flowers: male and female flowers grow on separate trees in hanging clusters.

Fruit: the wings, 2cm across, are set at an acute angle; pale brown when ripe, they remain on the tree after the leaves have fallen.

Ash-leaved Maple

NORWAY MAPLE

(Acer platanoides)

The Norway maple is found all over Europe (except the extreme north); grows to a height of 30m. It is often planted as a shelter belt and for shade and ornament, particularly in city streets (since it tolerates smoke).

Crown: tall, domed or spreading, and dense, often on a very short trunk.

Bark: smooth and grey-brown, with a network of shallow ridges.

Shoots: pinkish-brown.

Buds: egg-shaped, dark red or brown (at the tips of the branches).

Leaves: 5-lobed, with the tip and teeth of each lobe ending in long slender points; 12 by 15cm. Borne on long (15cm) slender stalks containing milky sap, the leaves open rusty red, becoming bright green above and

Norway Maple

winter

ripe fruit

paler beneath, and turning yellow then orange-brown before falling.

Flowers: grow in erect clusters of 30—40 that open before the leaves.

Fruit: the wings, 6—10cm across, are set at an obtuse angle; they ripen from yellow-green to brown.

Uses: the hard heavy fine-grained wood — white or greyish — is used for furniture and turned articles.

SYCAMORE

(Acer pseudoplatanus)

Growing wild in mountainous regions of southern and central Europe, the sycamore is widely planted for shelter, ornament, and timber (it has become naturalized in many parts); since it tolerates pollution, it is often grown in towns and cities. It reaches a height of 35m.

Crown: dense and broadly domed, with spreading branches.

Bark: smooth and grey, becoming pinkish-brown and flaking off in irregular plates.

Buds: green and egg-shaped; 8—12mm long.

Leaves: up to 18 by 26cm, divided into 5 pointed coarsely toothed lobes. Borne on reddish stalks, up to 15cm long, the leaves are orange or reddish when they first open, becoming deep green and matt above and pale blue-green beneath.

Flowers: grow in dense narrow hanging clusters of 50 to 100, 6—12cm long.

Fruit: the wings, about 3cm long and set at right angles, are green tinged with red, turning brown when the fruit is ripe.

Uses: the hard yellowish-white fine-grained timber is used for furniture, turned articles (bowls, spoons, etc.), carving, textile rollers, violins and other musical instruments, and veneers.

MONTPELIER MAPLE

(Acer monspessulanum)

This small maple, growing in dry hilly and rocky districts of southern Europe and western Asia, is sometimes planted for ornament in parks and gardens; it reaches a height of 15m.

Crown: dense and broadly domed.

Sycamore

Bark: dark grey to black, with vertical cracks.
Shoots: smooth, slender, and pale brown.
Buds: small (3mm), egg-shaped, and dark orange-brown.
Leaves: hard and leathery, 4 by 8cm, with 3 rounded untoothed lobes. Borne on orange-pink stalks, 4cm long, the leaves are bright green on opening, becoming dark green above and grey-blue beneath.
Flowers: grouped in flat-topped erect (later drooping) clusters.
Fruit: paired brown nutlets attached to parallel or overlapping wings—green or pinkish, each 1·2cm long and borne on a 4cm stalk.

flowers

fruit

Montpelier Maple

SMOOTH JAPANESE MAPLE *(Acer palmatum)*

Native to Japan and Korea, this species is widely planted in gardens as an ornamental small tree or shrub for its colourful foliage (there are many cultivated varieties); it grows to a height of 15m.
Crown: low and broadly domed, with spreading twisted branches.
Bark: smooth and brown.
Shoots: smooth and slender; dark red above, green beneath.

Buds: egg-shaped, green-and-red; 2—3mm long.
Leaves: divided into 5 to 7 long pointed lobes (each 7—9cm long) and borne on slender stalks, 3—5cm long. The basic type is bright green, but ornamental varieties are various shades of red (var. *atropurpureum* is bright red-purple to dark purple).
Flowers: purple-red, 6—8mm across, in small erect clusters of 12 to 15 on slender dark-red stalks, 4cm long.
Fruit: pale red, 2cm across, with the wings set at an obtuse angle; the fruits grow in erect bunches.

A beautiful orange-leaved variety of the Japanese maple.

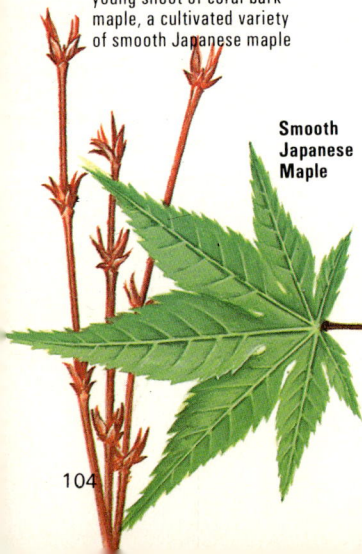

young shoot of coral bark maple, a cultivated variety of smooth Japanese maple

Smooth Japanese Maple

HORSE CHESTNUT FAMILY *(Hippocastanaceae)*

HORSE CHESTNUT
(Aesculus hippocastanum)

Native to the Balkans, this fast-growing impressive tree is very widely planted for ornament and shade; it withstands pollution and is naturalized in some parts of Europe. It reaches a height of 30m.

Crown: tall and domed, on a short thick trunk.

Bark: dark grey-brown or reddish-brown, flaking off in scales.

Shoots: stout; grey or pink-brown.

Buds: large and pointed (2·5 by 1·5cm), shiny dark red-brown, and sticky with resin.

Leaves: compound, with 5 to 7 toothed leaflets (up to 25 by 10cm), which are pointed and broadest near the tip, arising from the same point on the stout yellow-green stalk (up to 20cm long). Bright green at first, they become darker above, yellow-green beneath, and turn gold, orange, or scarlet in autumn; they leave horseshoe-shaped scars when they fall.

Flowers: 2cm across, with fringed white petals tinged with crimson or

winter

Horse Chestnut

yellow at the base; they grow in erect clusters, 15–30cm long.

Fruit: green, globular, and spiny, splitting when ripe (brown) to reveal 1 to 3 shiny brown seeds (conkers).

Uses: the soft white wood has been used for joinery, cabinetwork, turnery, etc.; the seeds provide fodder for cattle and horses in eastern Europe.

opening bud

fruit opening to show conker

bark of horse chestnut

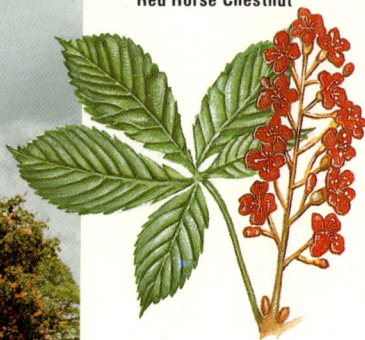

Red Horse Chestnut

The red horse chestnut is planted as an ornamental tree in parks and on roadsides.

RED HORSE CHESTNUT

(Aesculus x carnea)

This hybrid between the horse chestnut and the American red buckeye (*A. pavia*) is widely planted as an ornamental; reaches a height of 20m.

Buds: egg-shaped, 1·5—2·5cm, but not sticky.
Leaves: similar to those of the horse chestnut but the leaflets are darker, crinkled, sometimes shiny above, and have broader, more jagged, teeth.
Flowers: red, in erect clusters 12—20cm long.
Fruit: usually not spiny; each contains 2 to 3 small dull-brown seeds.

LIME FAMILY *(Tiliaceae)*

Small-leaved Lime

Most of the 300 to 400 species of this family are native to tropical and warm regions. The limes, widely distributed in northern temperate regions, all have small fragrant flowers (with 5 sepals, 5 petals, and many stamens) hanging in clusters from leafy strap-like bracts; they develop into nut-like fruits, each with 1 to 3 seeds. The soft white wood is used for carving, turnery, hat blocks, piano keys, and wood pulp.

SMALL-LEAVED LIME

(Tilia cordata)

Growing wild throughout Europe, the small-leaved lime is also widely planted for shade and ornament, especially in avenues; it grows to 30m.
Crown: tall, dense, and domed.
Bark: smooth and grey, becoming dark grey and cracked into plates.
Shoots: red above, olive beneath.
Buds: smooth, shiny dark red, and egg-shaped.
Leaves: heart-shaped, 4–7 by 3–5cm, with finely toothed margins. Borne on yellow-green or pinkish stalks 3·5cm long, they are dark shiny green above, and paler — with tufts of reddish hairs at the bases of the veins — beneath.
Flowers: white, growing in erect or spreading clusters of 4 to 15 from pale green bracts, 6cm long.
Fruit: small (6mm across), rounded, and smooth or indistinctly ribbed.

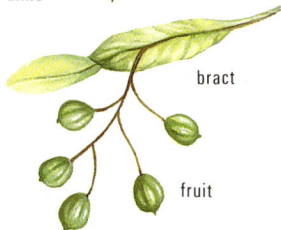

bract

Small-leaved Lime

bract

fruit

LARGE-LEAVED LIME

(Tilia platyphyllos)

Another widespread European lime (although not extending as far north as the small-leaved species), this tree is planted for ornament. It grows to a height of 40m.
Crown: tall and domed, with up-growing branches.
Shoots: reddish-green and hairy.
Leaves: rounded, with a pointed tip and sharply toothed margins; 6–15 by

winter

Large-leaved Lime

bract

fruit

6–15cm. Borne on hairy stalks, 2–5cm long, they are dark green and hairy above, and paler — with white hairs on the veins — beneath.
Flowers: yellowish-white, hanging in clusters of 3 to 4 from whitish-green bracts, 5–12cm long.
Fruit: rounded, 8–10mm across, each with 3 to 5 prominent ribs and densely covered with hairs.

COMMON LIME

(Tilia x europaea;
Tilia x vulgaris)

This tree — a hybrid between the small-leaved and large-leaved limes — is often planted for shade and ornament, especially in streets and avenues in north-west Europe; it produces suckers and reaches a height of 40m.
Crown: tall and domed, with up-turned branches (the lower branches are arched).
Bark: dull grey and smooth, becoming rough with a network of shallow ridges and (usually) bosses.
Shoots: green tinged with red.
Buds: reddish-brown and egg-shaped.
Leaves: heart-shaped, 6–10cm long, with toothed margins and an unequal base. Borne on green hairless stalks, 2–5cm long, they are dull green above, pale green and rather shiny beneath with tufts of buff or white hairs at the bases of the veins; the leaves turn yellow in autumn.
Flowers: yellowish-white, hanging

Common Lime

winter

bract

fruit

in clusters of 4 to 10 from yellow-green bracts.
Fruit: egg-shaped, downy, and slightly ribbed; 8mm across.
Uses: (timber) the fibrous inner bark has been used for ropes, matting, etc.

SILVER LIME

(Tilia tomentosa)

Native to south-east Europe (the Balkans) and south-west Asia, the silver lime is quite often planted for ornament; it grows to 30m.
Crown: broadly conical or domed, with steeply up-turned branches.
Bark: dark greenish with vertical markings, becoming grey with a network of flat ridges.
Shoots: whitish and densely downy, becoming dark grey-green above and bright green beneath.
Buds: egg-shaped and hairy, 6–8mm long; green and brown.

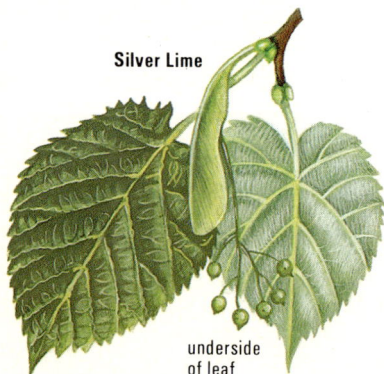

Silver Lime

underside
of leaf

Leaves: rounded, with a pointed tip, toothed margins, and an unequal base; 12 by 10cm. Borne on downy 5-cm stalks, the leaves are dark green and crinkled above, pale grey and downy beneath.

Flowers: yellow-white, growing in clusters of 6 to 10 from yellow-green bracts, 9 by 2cm.

Fruit: egg-shaped and warty, 6–10mm long.

Silver Lime

POMEGRANATE FAMILY *(Punicaceae)*

POMEGRANATE
(Punica granatum)

Originally from south-west Asia, this small, much-branched tree is now widely grown in southern Europe for its fruit (it is naturalized in some parts); the pomegranate is occasionally grown for its ornamental flowers in temperate regions. It reaches a height of 6m.

Shoots: angled and hairless.

Leaves: slender and shining bright green, 2–8cm long, growing on short stalks.

Flowers: orange-red and showy, 3–4cm across; the sepals are united in a tube from which 4 crumpled petals and many stamens emerge. Some ornamental varieties have double flowers.

Fruit: a large berry, 5–8cm across, with a brownish-red leathery skin enclosing a sweet or acid-tasting purple to white pulp divided into compartments containing many seeds.

Uses: the fruit is eaten raw and its juice can be drunk fresh or made into wine; the seeds are used in jams and syrups. The bark, rind, and roots of the tree were formerly used medicinally (especially as a worm powder).

ripe fruit

section through fruit

Pomegranate

MYRTLE FAMILY *(Myrtaceae)*

BLUE GUM
(Eucalyptus globulus)

This tall fast-growing evergreen from south Australia is widely planted in frost-free parts of Europe for ornament and timber; reaches a height of 40m.
Crown: conical or domed, high, and dense, on a straight cylindrical trunk.
Bark: a pale-brown outer bark flakes off to reveal patches of grey, brown, and white smooth inner bark.
Leaves: (mature) lance- or sickle-shaped, 10–30 by 3–8cm, glossy dark blue-green and dotted with glands; (young) oblong, 10–15cm long, and pointed at base and tip; pale greyish-blue to white.
Flowers: whitish, about 4cm across, and borne singly; the petals and sepals are united to form a beaked cap that splits to reveal numerous yellow stamens.
Fruit: large blackish top-shaped capsules, 1–1·5 by 1·5–3cm, with greyish-blue lids that open to release the seeds.
Uses: medicinal eucalyptus oil is obtained from the leaves.

CIDER GUM
(Eucalyptus gunnii)

Native to south Australia, the cider gum is the most commonly planted eucalyptus in north-west Europe, where it reaches a height of 20–30m.

Blue Gum

flower

young flower

old fruit

flower bud

110

Crown: conical at first, with upswept branches, becoming tall, domed, and heavily branched.

Bark: smooth and grey beneath pinkish-orange peeling strips.

Shoots: yellowish-white, covered with a pinkish-grey bloom.

Leaves: (mature) evergreen and oblong, 8–10 by 3–4cm, tapering to a point at the tip; borne on pale-yellow stalks 2·5cm long, these leaves are dark blue-grey above, yellow-green beneath, and smell of cider when crushed. Young leaves are rounded, 3–6cm across, and pale blue-grey.

Flowers: white and fluffy, in clusters of 3, opening from blue-white egg-shaped rimmed buds.

Fruit: white top-shaped flat-ended capsules, 5mm long.

flowers

Cider Gum

MYRTLE *(Myrtus communis)*

A dense much-branched evergreen shrub, the myrtle grows wild in dry sunny positions, woods, and thickets in the Mediterranean region; reaches a height of 5m. It is quite widely planted for ornament.

Shoots: downy.

Leaves: oval, 2–3 by 1·5cm, with a pointed base and tip. Dark green and leathery, the leaves are dotted with glands and are very aromatic when crushed.

Flowers: sweet-scented, 2cm across, with 5 white petals and numerous stamens. Opening from globular buds enclosed in 5 shiny brown sepals, the flowers grow on long stalks from the axils of the upper leaves.

Fruit: rounded purple-black berries, 6·5mm long.

Uses: the hard mottled wood is used for turned articles and charcoal; the leaves, flowers, and fruit yield an oil used in perfumery.

Myrtle

fruit

flower bud

DOGWOOD FAMILY *(Cornaceae)*

winter

Dogwood

DOGWOOD

(Cornus sanguinea)

Found throughout Europe (except the far north), the dogwood grows as a shrub or small tree in hedgerows, thickets, woods, and scrub. It prefers chalky soils and produces suckers freely; it reaches a height of 4m.
Bark: greenish-grey.
Shoots: dark red and very conspicuous in winter.
Buds: slender and scaleless.
Leaves: oval, 4–10cm long, with a pointed tip and prominent curved

veins. The leaves turn from pale green to dark red in autumn.
Flowers: small and white, with 4 wide-spreading petals, 4 sepals, and 4 stamens. The flowers grow in flat-topped clusters, 4–5cm across, at the tips of the branches.
Fruit: globular, 6–8mm across, ripening from green to shiny black. The bitter-tasting flesh encloses a hard stone containing 2 seeds.
Uses: the wood — tough, white, and smooth — was originally used to make skewers.

HEATHER FAMILY
(Ericaceae)

STRAWBERRY TREE

(Arbutus unedo)

The small evergreen strawberry tree grows naturally in thickets, woods, and dry rocky places of south and south-west Europe as far north as south-west Ireland; it is sometimes planted for shelter and ornament. It reaches a height of 12m.
Crown: low, dense, and rounded, with up-growing branches supported on a very short trunk.
Bark: dark reddish, later peeling off and forming grey-brown ridges.

Dogwood

ripe fruit

winter twig

Strawberry Tree

flowers and fruit

bark of strawberry tree

Shoots: hairy; pinkish above, pale green beneath.
Buds: small (1–2mm), purple-red, and sharply pointed.
Leaves: lance-shaped, with sharply toothed margins; 5–10 by 2–3cm. Borne on hairy pinkish stalks, 5–7mm long, the leaves are shiny dark green above, paler green beneath.
Flowers: white (tinged with green or pink) and flask-shaped, 8 by 8mm, growing in hanging clusters 5cm long. The flowers appear in autumn, at the same time as the ripe fruit from the previous year.
Fruit: rounded, 2cm across, with a rough warty skin, ripening from yellow to scarlet. Though edible, the fruit does not have a particularly pleasant flavour.
Uses: the reddish-brown wood is used for carving, charcoal, and fuel.

CYPRESS STRAWBERRY TREE
(Arbutus andrachne)

Similar to the previous species, this evergreen shrub or small tree of the eastern Mediterranean can be distinguished by the following features:
Bark: (trunk) orange-red, peeling off to reveal pinkish patches; (branches) yellow-green.
Shoots: hairless; yellow-green, becoming brown.
Leaves: oval, 5–10 by 4–5cm, with smooth margins.
Flowers: grow in erect clusters that appear in spring.
Fruit: small (8–12mm across) and orange, with a smooth skin.

bark of Cypress strawberry tree

Cypress Strawberry Tree

113

HONEYSUCKLE FAMILY *(Caprifoliaceae)*

ELDER *(Sambucus nigra)*

The elder grows throughout Europe as a shrub or small tree of woods, hedges, scrub, and waste ground; it reaches a height of 10m.

Crown: irregular and much-branched.

Bark: greyish-brown, with thick corky ridges and deep cracks.

Shoots: stout and grey, with corky pores and thick white pith.

Buds: scaly; brownish-red or purple.

Leaves: compound, with 2 to 3 pairs of leaflets and one terminal leaflet. Each leaflet is oval to lance-shaped, 3–9cm long, with sharply toothed margins and a pointed tip.

Flowers: small (5mm across) and creamy white, grouped into flat-topped clusters 10–20cm across.

Fruit: berry-like and juicy, in large clusters, ripening from green to black.

Uses: the fruit, rich in vitamin C, is made into wine, jam, and jelly; the flowers can also be brewed to make a beverage. The wood – hard, heavy, and whitish – is used for small articles.

GUELDER ROSE
(Viburnum opulus)

Native to Europe, the small guelder rose grows in woodlands, scrub, hedgerows, and thickets; it reaches a height of 4–5m. Cultivated forms, planted for their flowers, are sterile.

Crown: spreading.

Shoots: smooth and angled.

Buds: greenish-yellow and scaly.

Leaves: 3- to 5-lobed, 5–8cm long, with deeply toothed margins and 2 glands at the base. Borne on greenish-red stalks, 3–4cm long, each with pointed stipules at its base, the leaves are downy at first, becoming smooth above and turning scarlet in autumn.

Flowers: white, in dense flat-topped clusters 5–10cm across. The outer flowers are large (2cm across) and sterile; the inner ones are smaller (6–8mm across) and fertile.

Fruit: red, translucent, and berry-like, 8mm across.

Elder

ripe fruit

Guelder Rose

WAYFARING TREE
(Viburnum lantana)

The wayfaring tree is found over most of Europe (except the extreme north), growing at the edges of woods, in thickets, and in hedges, especially on chalk or limestone soils; reaches a height of 6m.
Shoots: covered with greyish down.
Buds: lack scales.
Leaves: heart-shaped and wrinkled, 5–12cm long, with toothed margins and densely covered with down on the lower surface; they are borne on short downy stalks.
Flowers: all are white, small (6mm across), and fertile, grouped in flat-topped clusters, 6–10cm across.
Fruit: small, oval, and flattened, in flat-topped or domed clusters, ripening unevenly from green to red and finally black.

Wayfaring Tree

flower bud in winter

ripe fruit

STORAX FAMILY *(Styracaceae)*

STORAX *(Styrax japonica)*

This slender-branched shrub or small tree is native to east and south-east Europe and south-west Asia; grows to a height of 7m.
Leaves: broad and oval, 2·5–6cm long, with a rounded or slightly pointed tip and covered with white starlike branched hairs.
Flowers: white, 1·6–2cm long, with

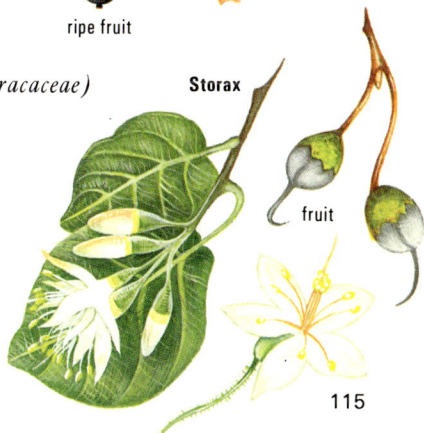
Storax

fruit

115

5 pointed spreading petals surrounding 10–16 hairy orange-tipped stamens joined at their bases; a long style protrudes from the stamen's centre.

Fruit: rounded, greyish, and dry, with a persistent style at the tip and cupped in a yellowish-green lobed calyx; encloses 1 to 2 seeds.

Uses: the source of an aromatic gum, storax, used in medicine and perfumery.

SNOWBELL TREE
(Styrax officinalis)

Native to China and Japan, this small hardy tree makes an attractive flowering ornamental tree in gardens; it reaches a height of 11m.

Crown: dense and rounded, with spreading branches.

Bark: grey, with pinkish vertical markings, later developing thick ridges between orange cracks.

Shoots: slender, brownish speckled with black, and rather downy.

Buds: small (2–4mm long), narrow, and pointed; pale brown-green and downy, with black powdery warts.

Leaves: oval, 6–8cm long, with wavy margins and tapering to a point at tip and base (which is wedge-shaped). Borne on short (2–6mm) yellowish-green stalks, the leaves are shiny green above, and paler beneath.

Flowers: white and bell-like, with 5 oval petals (12mm long) and pale-orange stamens bunched together; the flowers hang in clusters of 3–4 on slender stalks, 2–4cm long.

Fruit: globular (1·5cm long), smooth, and greenish-grey, cupped in a persistent star-like calyx of rounded bright-green purple-tipped sepals.

OLIVE FAMILY
(Oleaceae)

This widely distributed family of trees and shrubs (400 to 500 species) includes many ornamental trees (such as the lilac and jasmine) as well as the economically important olive and ash. Their flowers usually contain only 2 stamens.

OLIVE *(Olea europaea)*

A slow-growing long-lived evergreen, the olive has been widely cultivated for fruit since ancient times in its native Mediterranean region; reaches a height of 15m. It grows wild in dry rocky places and is also planted in gardens for shade.

bark of olive

Snowbell Tree

fruit

Crown: spreading (bushy in wild forms), supported on a twisted gnarled trunk.
Bark: smooth and grey.
Shoots: covered with silvery scales.
Leaves: leathery and lance-shaped, 2–8cm long, dark green above and silvery-grey beneath. Wild trees often have small oval leaves.
Flowers: small and white, each with 2 yellow-tipped stamens, growing in dense clusters in the axils of the leaves. Some flowers have no pistils.
Fruit: egg-shaped, 1–3·5cm long, containing a single large seed; olives

Olive trees in a grove in southern Europe. The fruit is picked in autumn.

ripen from green to black or brownish-green.
Uses: the fruit is used as food and yields a high-quality oil (olive oil) used in cooking, medicine (as a lubricant, in ointments, and as a mild laxative), and in soap-making; the residue of the fruit (after the oil has been extracted) is used as cattle food. The wood, which is very hard, is used for carving, cabinetwork, fuel, and charcoal.

Olive

unripe fruit

ripe fruit

MANNA or FLOWERING ASH

(Fraxinus ornus)

The manna ash is native to south, south-east, and central Europe, where it grows in dry rocky regions, woods, and thickets; reaches a height of 20m. It is widely planted as an ornamental in parks, and is cultivated for commercial purposes in Italy.

Crown: rounded, with curving branches.

Bark: grey and very smooth.

Shoots: olive-green.

Buds: domed and densely covered with grey down; enclosed in 2 dark outer scales.

Leaves: compound, 25–30cm long, with 2 to 4 pairs of leaflets and one terminal leaflet. The leaflets (10 by 3·5cm) are stalked, lance-shaped, irregularly toothed, and covered with brownish or white down on the lower surface.

Flowers: white and fragrant, with very narrow 6-mm long petals, growing in dense conical clusters, 15 by 20cm, at the tips of the branches.

Fruit: slender wings ('keys'), 1·5–2·5cm long, each with a seed at its base. The keys hang in bunches and ripen from green to brown.

Uses: the branches yield a sap (manna), which hardens to form a gum used in pharmacy.

Manna Ash

bark of manna ash

Manna Ash

flowers

fruit

COMMON ASH

(Fraxinus excelsior)

Widely distributed in Europe and south-west Asia, the common ash is found in woods and scrub (it grows particularly well on moist alkaline soils); reaches a height of 40m. It is valued for its timber and also grown for ornament in parks, churchyards, etc.

Crown: tall and rounded, with steeply up-growing branches.

Bark: pale grey; smooth at first, it later develops a network of ridges.

Shoots: stout; greenish-grey with white markings.

Buds: conspicuously black, squat, and angled.

Leaves: compound, 20—35cm long, with 4 to 6 pairs of leaflets and one terminal leaflet. The leaflets, up to 12cm long, are stalkless (or nearly so) and pointed, with sharply toothed margins; dull green above and pale and downy beneath, they turn yellow in autumn.

Flowers: usually, male and female flowers grow on separate trees, but some trees bear both male and female flowers and others have hermaphrodite flowers. The flowers of both sexes are small and purplish, growing in small dense clusters that appear well before the leaves.

Fruit: strap-shaped keys, 2·5—5cm long, each with a notched tip. They ripen from shiny deep green to brown and remain on the tree after the leaves have fallen.

Uses: the pale tough elastic timber is used for sports equipment (oars, hockey sticks, etc.), tool handles, furniture, walking sticks, pegs, etc.; it also makes good fuel and charcoal.

natural distribution of common ash

male flowers

female flowers

Common Ash

fruit

winter buds

winter

119

GLOSSARY

acorn: the fruit of oak trees: a nut partly enclosed in a cuplike husk.

aril: a fleshy, often brightly coloured, covering around certain seeds, e.g. of the yew and spindle tree.

axil: the angle between the stalk of a leaf and the stem from which it grows.

berry: a fleshy, often edible, fruit containing many seeds.

boss: a rounded protuberance, e.g. on a tree trunk or cone scale.

bract: 1. a small leaflike structure in some trees, e.g. limes, in the axil of which a flower or flower cluster grows. 2. a small scale at the base of a cone scale in some conifers, e.g. silver fir.

broad-leaved tree: a tree that produces flowers (which develop into fruits containing seeds) and has leaves that are usually broader and flatter than those of conifers.

bud: a structure protected by overlapping scales that remains on the tree throughout winter and develops into a new shoot the following spring: a means of identification in some trees.

calyx: the sepals of a flower, collectively. The calyx may be a tube of united sepals or consist of separate sepals.

capsule: a dry fruit, e.g. of willows and poplars, that splits open when ripe to release its seeds.

catkin: a cluster of small one-sexed flowers often lacking stalks. Catkins are usually long and hanging but may be small and erect.

compound: describing a leaf made up of several leaflets arising from the same leafstalk.

cone: the reproductive structure of pines and other conifers, made up of scales. After fertilization female cones become woody or leathery and their scales bear seeds. Some broad-leaved trees, e.g. alder, have cone-like fruits.

conifer: a tree, usually evergreen, that produces its seeds in cones and has needle-like or scale-like leaves.

crown: the part of a tree formed by the branches and leaves, as distinct from the trunk. The shape of the crown aids in the identification of some trees.

deciduous: describing trees that shed all their leaves together at the same time of the year and have bare branches in winter.

drupe: a fleshy fruit, of e.g. the walnut, containing a hard stone in which is a single seed.

evergreen: describing trees that grow and shed their leaves continuously, so that their branches are never bare.

family: a group of related plants that are divided into different genera.

fertilization: the union of a male sex cell from a pollen grain and a female sex cell in an ovule, resulting in the formation of fruit and seed.

flower: the part of a broad-leaved tree or palm that contains the reproductive structures. **Male flowers** have functional stamens but lack a pistil; **female flowers** have a functional pistil but no stamens.

fluted: describing a tree trunk that has rounded grooves running from base to tip.

fruit: the dry or fleshy structure of broad-leaved trees and palms that encloses the seed(s) and develops from a fertilized ovary.

genus (pl. **genera**): a group of closely related species that belong to the same family and have many features in common.

hardwood: the wood obtained

from a broad-leaved tree, or the tree itself.

heartwood: the wood at the centre of a tree trunk.

hermaphrodite: describing a flower that has both male and female organs.

inflorescence: a group of flowers borne on a single main stalk and arranged in a particular way.

kernel: the seed of nuts and some other fruits, which contains a large food store and is usually edible.

leaflet: any of the small blades that together make up a compound leaf.

midrib: the largest vein of a leaf, usually running through the centre of the leaf from base to tip.

nut: a dry fruit consisting of a hard shell surrounding a single, usually edible kernel.

nutlet: a small nutlike fruit or part of a fruit containing a single seed, as in maples and hawthorns.

ovary: part of the pistil of a flower that contains the ovule(s) and develops into the fruit after fertilization.

ovule: the structure inside the pistil of a flower that contains the female sex cell and develops into the seed after fertilization.

palm: a treelike flowering plant that does not produce true wood.

persistent: describing parts of a flower, e.g. the style, that remain after the rest of the flower has withered, forming part of the fruit.

petal: one of the parts of a flower that surround the stamens and pistil. In insect-pollinated flowers petals are usually brightly coloured.

pistil: the female organ of a flower, in which, after fertilization, the seeds are formed.

pod: the long fruit of leguminous plants, e.g. laburnum, acacia. It contains many seeds, which are released when the pod splits open.

pollen: minute grains containing male sex cells and produced by the stamens of a flower.

pollination: the transfer of pollen from the stamens to the stigma, either of the same flower or of two different flowers.

rootstock: a rooted stem of a tree on which stems from another tree are grafted.

sapwood: the outer wood of a tree trunk, just beneath the bark.

seed: the structure that contains the embryo plant and its food store, is surrounded by a hard protective seed coat, and develops from a fertilized ovule.

sepal: one of the parts of a flower that surround the petals and together form the calyx. Sepals are usually green and protect the flower in the bud.

shoot: the youngest part of a branch: a means of identification in some trees.

softwood: the wood obtained from a conifer, or the conifer itself.

species: a group of individuals that are essentially alike and able to interbreed to produce more of the same kind. The blue gum is one species; the cider gum is another in the same genus.

stamen: the male organ of a flower, at the tip of which the pollen is produced.

stigma: the part of the female organ of a flower, at the tip of the style, on which pollen is deposited.

stipule: a small leaflike structure at the base of the leafstalk in some trees, e.g. those of the rose family, usually occurring in pairs.

style: the elongated part of the female organ (pistil) of a flower, between the ovary and the stigma.

sucker: a shoot that grows from a stem or root below ground and by which a tree can reproduce itself vegetatively (i.e. asexually).

Index

(English Names)

The Publishers wish to thank the following for their kind help in supplying photographs for this book:

A-Z Botanical Collection, page 8, Maurice Nimmo, pages 28, 32, 45, 46, 50, 55, 58, 67 bottom, 89, 90, 94, 104, 106, 113 top & bottom. Biofotos, pages 105, 116. British Tourist Authority, page 24. Michael Chinery, page 82. Sonia Halliday, page 30, 40, 63, 69. Brian Hawkes, page 67 top. Ken Merrylees, pages 27, 33, 48, 56, 57, 68, 71 bottom, 75, 81 top & bottom. P. Morris, pages 36, 60, 71 top, 117. NHPA, page 39. Oleg Polunin, pages 95 top & bottom, 96, 119. ZEFA (UK) Ltd, pages 19, 37, 98. Picture Research: Penny Warn.